What people are saying about ...

When "I Do" Becomes "I Don't"

"This book is excellent! Laura's ability to answer the complex questions associated with separation and divorce with nonjudgmental biblical insight is admirable. Anyone coping with separation or divorce will benefit from her helpful and encouraging approach."

Gigi Graham, author and speaker

"With great empathy and an insight born of personal experience, Laura Petherbridge's book provides sensitive and practical help for those facing or recovering from the tragedy and trauma of divorce."

Archibald D. Hart, PhD, FPPR, senior professor of psychology and dean emeritus of the Graduate School of Psychology, Fuller Theological Seminary

"I'm glad Laura Petherbridge wrote this book. She has carefully cataloged many of the big questions related to separation and divorce and organized them into an easy-to-read and very usable guide to surviving and healing."

Steve Grissom, founder and president of DivorceCare

"Laura has taken the pain of her past and used it for personal growth. Her inspiring story made me cry, laugh, but most importantly, challenged me to move forward in faith; knowing that God will take the worst things in my life and use them for His good! I highly recommend her book to anyone who is seeking to GROW through his or her separation or divorce."

Tom Whiteman, PhD, president and founder of Fresh Start Seminars

"In the fourteen years that my wife, Beverly, and I have known Laura Petherbridge, we have witnessed her compassion for those in the midst of separation or divorce. *When "I Do" Becomes "I Don't"* offers sound wisdom for the complex financial issues associated with divorce, as well as helpful insights on a variety of other topics. I highly recommend this resource for pastors, leaders, and individuals."

Howard Dayton, cofounder of Crown Financial Ministries

"Do you have questions about your divorce—why it happened? How to overcome the anger or pain? What to do about the behavior of your ex-spouse? You have questions—Laura has answers."

Dick Purnell, author and founder of Single Life Resources,
a Division of Campus Crusade For Christ

"*When "I Do" Becomes "I Don't"* is a much-needed resource in today's world and provides a lifeline to people in pain and a way back to hope."

Pam Farrel, author and speaker

"Laura Petherbridge captures the thoughts, questions, and unique difficulties associated with separation and divorce in her book *When "I Do" Becomes "I Don't."* I know from personal experience how lonely and difficult the process of separation and divorce can be, and that's why I highly recommend this resource for anyone in similar circumstances."

Kim Hill, Dove award-winning recording artist, worship leader, and author

"The divorce experience is filled with lots of questions, and Laura has answers. Like a comforting conversation over coffee with a trusted friend, this book will help get you through—and beyond—divorce."

Ron L. Deal, president of Successful Stepfamilies
and author of *The Smart Stepfamily*

"*When "I Do" Becomes "I Don't"* is a wise and practical guide to navigating the rapids of divorce country. With personal insight and guidance, Laura will help readers to make wise and positive choices that will enable them to rebuild their lives in the land beyond divorce. She opens a window of hope for every reader and applies spiritual direction to this new journey."

Jim Smoke, speaker, life coach, and author of *Growing Through Divorce*

"*When "I Do" Becomes "I Don't"* provides practical wisdom from a seasoned divorce-recovery expert. Laura's easy-to-follow question-and-answer format, plus an informative list of Dos and Don'ts, reveals the real-life issues surrounding separation and divorce. Her beautiful devotional prayers at the end of each chapter will provide comfort for any reader."

Joseph Warren Kniskern, Esq., attorney, family mediator,
and author of *When the Vow Breaks* and *Making a NEW Vow*

When
"I Do"
Becomes
"I Don't"

When "I Do" Becomes "I Don't"

Practical Steps for Healing During Separation & Divorce

Laura Petherbridge

transforming lives together

WHEN "I DO" BECOMES "I DON'T"
Published by David C. Cook
4050 Lee Vance View
Colorado Springs, CO 80918 U.S.A.

David C. Cook Distribution Canada
55 Woodslee Avenue, Paris, Ontario, Canada N3L 3E5

David C. Cook U.K., Kingsway Communications
Eastbourne, East Sussex BN23 6NT, England

David C. Cook and the graphic circle C logo
are registered trademarks of Cook Communications Ministries.

LCCN 2008927686
ISBN 978-1-4347-6876-6

© 2008 Laura Petherbridge
www.LauraPetherbridge.com

Originally published as *When Your Marriage Dies*
ISBN 0-7814-4149-8
© 2005 Life Journey

The Team: Susan Tjaden, Amy Kiechlin, and Jaci Schneider
Cover and Interior Design: Greg Jackson, ThinkPen Design
Cover Image: © Digital Vision, Getty Images

Printed in the United States of America
Second Edition 2008

1 2 3 4 5 6 7 8 9 10

To Steve—
No one has ever loved me as you do.

and

Carol Young—
When I was drowning in sorrow,
God used you to hold my head above the water.

Contents

Acknowledgments

A special thank you ...

To my friend and author Eva Marie Everson for your inspiration and knowledge. You pushed me out of the nest and encouraged me to believe that I could write.

To the remarkable ladies in my writers' group: LeAnne Benfield Martin, Laurie Fuller, Nicole Smith, Gloria Spencer, and Ruth Trippy. I'm wholeheartedly grateful for your generous gift of hours of critiquing and editing. Your honesty produced a better manuscript and pressed me to do my best.

To the precious ones who shared their painful divorce experiences. Take comfort in knowing your suffering will help others encountering the same sorrow.

To my husband, Steve, for your faith, encouragement, and affirmation.

To faithful friends who prayed for my ministry and this book. Not until heaven will you know the full impact of your devoted prayers.

To Mary McNeil and Susan Tjaden, my editors, and David C. Cook for believing in this book and understanding the pain of divorce.

To God, who extended grace and bound up the wounds of this shattered woman. You alone take something bad and turn it around for the good of others.

Foreword

One of my daughters is a consummate question-asker. From the day she began forming even the simplest words, she has posed a constant stream of the "why," "what," and "how" questions.

I love her deeply, but when I get tired, distracted, or just overwhelmed with the nonstop pace of her questioning, you know what happens—I tune her out. Mind you, this is not a good parenting technique, and I do my best to avoid it, but it helps me illustrate something you'll go through if you are facing separation or divorce.

You, too, will become a fountain of questions, even if you are not wired like my daughter. Important questions. Profound questions. Urgent questions. Imponderable questions.

You will likely find that the people who love you most will begin to tune you out as well. It's not that they don't care, but the sheer number and magnitude of your questions overwhelm them. They also feel ill-equipped to offer answers because the issues are overwhelmingly complex.

That's why I'm glad Laura Petherbridge wrote this book and that you are reading it.

She has carefully cataloged many of the big questions related to separation and divorce and organized them into an easy-to-read and very usable guide to surviving and healing.

Laura's own experience with divorce and her many years of divorce ministry makes her qualified to help answer the questions that are pressing in on you. You'll find wisdom and actionable information in this book. Most important, Laura will show you how to connect with God to find the answers to the questions that only He can answer.

This is a good book to share with the people who love you and are trying to help you. They'll better understand the pain, pressure, and problems you are facing once they've read it.

Follow Laura's advice. She's pointing you toward the kind of healing and recovery that many people never find after divorce. There is hope for your future!

Steve Grissom
Founder and President, DivorceCare
www.DivorceCare.org

Preface

If you are reading this book, chances are you've either found yourself in a dead or dying marriage, or you are close to a loved one facing that situation. And you've probably quickly realized that a world of difference sits between having opinions about separation or divorce and finding yourself in a whole new situation where easy answers play hard to get.

Depending on your unique situation, you may find that some chapters in this book are quite painful to read. Facing a deep sense of loss, for example, is not easy. And most likely you are experiencing financial challenges you never thought you'd encounter—such as paying an attorney and working through child-support issues.

Marriage-related suffering will likely cause you to examine what you really believe about God. The author is a Christian; therefore, her source of strength is Jesus Christ. However, you may find yourself asking, "Does God exist? Who am I? Why did He allow this to happen to me? How do I cope with forgiveness? Who am I in relationship to God?"

But regardless of your religious beliefs, separation and divorce are a perplexing maze. No question you ask is foolish, outrageous, or unique. Family and friends may not understand what's happening, nor the very personal choices you'll have to make as you sort out who you are going to be—or why.

THE STRUCTURE OF THIS BOOK

This book will help you find healing by sharing answers to questions most frequently asked in divorce-recovery groups. Because the pain associated with divorce is often so severe, a person sometimes can't find the strength to pray. Therefore, the author has included a heartfelt prayer at the end of each chapter. We'll address practical issues such as the kinds of losses you're experiencing, the stages of grief and recovery, dealing with an ex-spouse, and more. We've included beneficial action steps along the way to help you move from discouragement to restoration.

Much of the information is presented in a question-answer format. You may not agree with the answers to every question, and that's expected. Obviously, no one can answer each question perfectly, and every circumstance is somewhat unique. But ask yourself, "Why am I rejecting this answer? Is it because I don't want to believe it's true?"

Please understand that you may need to read a few chapters to find the answer to your inquiry. Many times the way a question is asked determines the chapter in which it appears. However, a question may also fall into more than one category; so if you don't find one similar to yours, keep reading. For example, a problem with children's visitation could fall into several categories, including children, legal and financial, or the holidays.

As you think through the questions at the end of each chapter, on your own or in a group, you'll have an exciting and significant choice to make. Will you wrestle with the deeper issues, or will you gloss over them at a distance? Some of the questions may be easy to answer, but others may touch a deep chord in you that brings tears and causes other raw emotions such as anger and fear to surface. But you will find healing—and part of that healing process includes finding people who will love you and stand by you, people you can love and support in turn. That's the power of community.

Prayerfully consider what God may want to reveal to you through these questions and ensuing discussions. Try to open yourself up to the feedback of others who are also dealing with separation/divorce issues.

Perhaps you will discover that you would benefit from the services of a trained Christian counselor, if you are not already seeing one. If so, don't hold back. God ministers to us in many ways—including trained professionals. Depression, thoughts of suicide, and issues of low self-esteem are particularly challenging issues.

You may not personally be going through a divorce, but I'm almost certain you have a friend, family member, or coworker who is experiencing this loss. Therefore, we have included an appendix for family member and friends.

You may be a pastor or leader in your church who desires to learn what you can do to lower the divorce rate. The inspirational appendix on divorce prevention provides unique insights on why divorce occurs and what your church can do to strengthen the institution of marriage.

And for those who desire to help others in the midst of divorce, we have included an appendix with information on starting a divorce-recovery ministry.

May you will find this book beneficial as you walk through the journey of recovery.

The author has chosen to be vulnerable in many parts of this book. Learn from her and from other people in your life. And embrace God. He is, after all, in the personal healing business. Best of all, He loves you. You are not alone!

INTRODUCTION

My Marriage Died, But I Can't Find the Funeral

LAURA'S STORY

No one ever told me grief felt so much like fear.

C. S. LEWIS

I hadn't expected Saturday, April 7, 1984, to be anything but ordinary. I was getting all "gussied up" to attend a women's luncheon with my mom and some friends. But I never made it to the event. I started crying that morning—and didn't stop for a very long time.

Looking back, I now see many obvious indications that something was terribly wrong with my marriage, but at the time, I didn't recognize them. The change in my husband's personality was evident that day as it had been for several months. While toweling my hair dry, I whispered, "Lord, show me what's wrong."

Before I could stop myself, I blurted out, "Is there someone else?"

My husband hesitated, and then said, "There could be."

"There could be?" I snapped. "I need a yes or no."

"Yes," he admitted.

Furious, I repeatedly screamed, "How could you? How could you do this?" Stunned by my outburst, he left the house. I wept as I waited for my friend to pick me up for the luncheon. When she saw me, her smile dissolved. I fell into her arms, sobbing, "He's having an affair." She led me to a chair where I sat zombie-like as she dried my hair and helped me to dress.

The pain of his confession hit me in waves, and each time a wave crashed over me, I'd burst into another crying jag. My friend held me and whispered, "Honey, it will be okay." But deep inside, I knew life would never be the same.

That was the day my marriage died.

Weeks passed in a dull haze, and I fervently prayed that I would wake from the nightmare. In shock, I spent the following months barely able to function, coasting through daily tasks, and begging God to heal our marriage.

All I wanted to do was sleep. Eating was nearly impossible. To numb the pain, I began drinking heavily. This huge mistake fueled my deepening depression. It was as if I were descending into a big, bottomless hole. In my journal I wrote, "My prayer is that I can get through the day without such a deep depression that I'm driven to sin. Oh God, help me. I'm falling ... falling ... falling.... I feel as if there is no hope. Please, God, tell me what to do."

As life seemed to unfold perfectly for everyone else, I stumbled through the next few months making one mistake after another in an effort to simply survive. My mental state and emotions fluctuated wildly. "Lord, I wish I knew what to do with my life. If only I could get some self-worth back.... I feel like the whole thing is my fault. I never realized my husband was so unhappy. Is it really over? Oh God, help me."

In time the fog lifted, and I unwillingly faced reality: My husband wanted out. Our marriage covenant was broken. There was nothing more I could do to save our relationship.

Now I must get on with my life, I told myself. But how? How do you put a puzzle back together when half the pieces are missing? How do you go shopping when you can't remember what you need to buy? How do you brush your teeth when you can't even find the sink? How do you start over when grief, fear, and anger cripple your thinking and your ability to focus?

Although friends and family tried to help, I sank deeper into despair. No one seemed to understand the tremendous sorrow I was experiencing. My church friends tried to comfort me, but at the end of the day they returned home to loving families. How could they understand my loneliness?

On the gloomy February day of my divorce, I wore a black wool suit to court. I was going to a funeral; I might as well look the part. I went alone, assuming that the grueling elements of the ordeal were over. I was wrong. My tears began in the judge's chambers and continued throughout the proceedings. Afterward the noisy, congested hallways complicated my attempt to exit the building. Confused and embarrassed, I finally bolted for the nearest door, desperate for fresh air.

As the days passed, Philippians 4:6–7 became my comfort. "Do not be anxious about anything, but in everything, by prayer and petition, with thanksgiving, present your requests to God. And the peace of God, which transcends all understanding, will guard your hearts and your minds in Christ Jesus." In my Bible next to this verse I wrote, "January 1985—Oh God, when will the pain be over and a purpose clear?"

In prayer I laid each tear and every feeling of anxiety, dread, and frustration at His feet. I clung to the hope that "this too shall pass" and believed God would one day do something worthwhile with the horrible mess of my divorce. As I learned to surrender the situation to God, my journal entries began to express a glimmer of hope. "The pain is still overwhelming, but I know You won't leave me, Lord.... I'm going to trust You.... With God's help, I'm going to learn how to be a single Christian."

I remember the first night I realized I had gone a full day without crying—a milestone in my healing.

Several months afterward, women in similar situations began calling me. They had gotten my name from a friend or church, and we would chat. Surprisingly, this was therapeutic for me. I felt productive as I focused on someone else's problems and not my own. How refreshing!

That was more than twenty years ago. For many years, I've led a divorce-recovery ministry and conducted seminars to help people cope with the aftermath of a failed marriage.

My own experience was similar to a plane crash—a catastrophic, immediate loss. But your marriage may have died slowly, as if contaminated by a lingering cancer. Regardless of the cause of death, the needs, fears, losses, and confusion form consistent and recognizable patterns that I see over and over as I lead divorce-recovery workshops across the country.

After years of assisting others through separation and divorce, I have seen the trauma strike emotionally, physically, spiritually, and mentally. I've seen women cry rivers of mascara and men sob like children. I've held more weeping people than I ever dreamed would come across my path.

But I've also seen people triumph over divorce. During a recent social event, I watched former students joke and laugh, when months earlier that behavior would have seemed unthinkable for them. They made the commitment to grow through the pain instead of letting it destroy them. They learned how to comfort and encourage each other.

I've also watched their children recover emotional health and grow spiritually. Before the divorce, many of these kids had no knowledge of a God who cared for them with an everlasting, passionate love. But because Mom or Dad became emotionally and spiritually stable, so did they.

It's been a joy to later celebrate with former students as they entered a new marriage with a wonderful spouse. The reward comes in seeing them choose to do the hard relational work necessary to enjoy fruitful and healthy lives. These blessings and many more give purpose to my own painful experience.

1

Stop the Roller Coaster!

THE STAGES OF LOSS

I can stand what I know. It's what I don't know that frightens me.
FRANCES NEWTON

"I've lost everything," the young woman lamented. "Will my life ever be normal again?"

Although many years had passed since my own divorce, I understood her intense emotions. While comforting her, I assured her she eventually would find a new sense of normal. But even that new standard wouldn't be in place for a while.

Most people are unaware that separation and divorce involve several stages of loss. These stages don't necessarily arrive in sequence—slipping back and forth through the process is typical. In time, if this young woman walks through the grief and not around it, she'll recover.

Most of us tend to want to rush through or numb our pain in an effort to get over our grief as quickly as possible. This is natural. Who likes pain? But rushing our healing is unwise and carries long-term consequences.

When you suffer a severe loss, your body and mind need to mourn in order to heal. If you don't allow yourself that necessary time to grieve, but instead try to anesthetize your sorrow with new relationships or other numbing agents, you jeopardize the healing process. You must choose whether to work through grief or to avoid it. The decision you make will affect your future for a long time.

Every circumstance surrounding divorce is different. If you had a violent or abusive marriage, you may experience a sense of relief instead of sorrow when it ends. But you will still need to grieve the death of your dream for what your marriage should have been. If you stayed in an unhappy marriage for many years, you run a greater risk of moving on too quickly following your divorce. After years of emotional numbness, the thought of starting life over again may seem invigorating. But if you don't discover how and why you married your ex-spouse—the red flags present during dating and what happened to destroy the marriage—you may repeat the same mistake. I once met a woman who married the same man three times. Granted, each had a different social security number, but they were the same person inside. She hadn't taken the time to learn why she gravitated to a certain type of man.

Elisabeth Kubler-Ross in her book *On Death and Dying* was one of the first people to share the theory that grief comes in stages. People tend to view grief stages as a "to do" list that can be accomplished in a few weeks or months. But you can't hurry or predict the process. It doesn't always follow the same pattern, and just when you think you've conquered one stage, it may recur. I frequently hear people say, "I thought I was over my anger, and I was shocked when something triggered it again." Knowing beforehand that these emotions will resurface should reassure you that you aren't abnormal or losing your mind.

THE STAGES OF GRIEF

SHOCK AND DENIAL: "THIS CAN'T BE HAPPENING TO ME."

During my separation, I kept thinking, *I can't believe I'm going through this. This isn't happening.* I refused to believe it. Certainly my husband would come to his senses, and the whole episode would be forgotten. The shock resonated so greatly that I couldn't concentrate or think clearly. I'd walk into a store and forget why I was there, and while driving, I'd miss a familiar road. Ordinary tasks became huge challenges. And when reality crashed through my wall of denial, I'd mumble to myself, "God will fix this, I just know it. He hates divorce, and so do I."

Our minds have a built-in numbing mechanism that allows us to process a catastrophe gradually. We can't grasp the devastation all at once. Initially, denial is normal, but you must be careful not to linger in it too long. Your healing begins as you accept reality.

Sadly, I've met men and women who are still hanging on to the dream of their marriage ten to fifteen years after their divorce—long after the ex-spouse has remarried another person and become unavailable.

ANGER: "I COULD KILL MY SPOUSE!"

My first husband and I owned a beautiful antique wooden cane. If you twisted the top and bottom while pulling it apart, you'd discover a sword hidden inside. During my divorce, I would imagine myself wielding that sword, slashing through artwork and linens in our once-shared bedroom. Thoughts of violence, even though unfulfilled, alarmed me. Before this time, I'd never dreamed of severely hurting anyone or anything.

I was riding an emotional roller coaster. One minute I'd want to hug my husband, and the next moment I'd want to punch him. I had never encountered rage within myself until divorce assaulted my life. But there it was, in living color—ricocheting relentlessly through my mind, demanding attention. Inside I was screaming, *How could you do this to me?* I had chosen marriage, but divorce was being decided for me. I no longer had control over my own life, and I felt violated. This wasn't the life I signed up for.

The embarrassment of going out in public also infuriated me. My mind was plagued with tormenting thoughts—*What will people think of me? Will they suppose it was my fault or that I wasn't a good wife? Do they think I'm a bad Christian?*

Your anger might be different. Your spouse may have refused to get help for his or her addiction, and now you are left feeling like the guilty one. Or you may have put your ex-spouse through college, but now your checkbook is stripped bare. God understands our anger when we've been hurt or rejected; it's a natural response.

Repressing anger is just as dangerous as acting on it because stuffing rage causes it to build until it destroys you and others. Fury turned inward leads to depression, bitterness, and resentment—and occasionally to violence.

God understands our anger and doesn't judge us for it. However, whether anger has to do with finances, children, housing, or other typical divorce issues, you must deal with it appropriately. Many people never move past resentment and the rut of revenge. The tragic consequences can be seen in health and financial problems, mental instability, and/or the emotional devastation of children.

BARGAINING: "I'LL DO ANYTHING."

During this stage, the injured spouse may promise to overlook the affair, drinking, abuse, pornography, gambling, drugs, or whatever.

You may be willing to compromise dignity and integrity if that means restoring some normalcy to your marriage. You may even shoulder the blame for your spouse's misdeeds (it wouldn't have happened if you'd been more attentive, attractive, a better housekeeper, and so on) if that means keeping the relationship intact. You may even agree to act as if "it" never happened.

Bargaining your way to marital reconciliation rarely works for long. The serious and complicated issues that damaged the marriage will continue to erode trust, love, and respect. And when a second separation results, the blow is even more severe.

Deep inside, you know it's unwise and unrealistic to cling to a person who wants out of the marriage. True marital restoration takes hard work by both parties. (See chapter 5.) If your spouse isn't willing to get counseling with you or isn't willing to work on the marriage, then you come to a point where you must accept the inevitable.

Bargaining to save your marriage is not only unrealistic, it can be dangerous. If your spouse is physically abusive, you need to seek help immediately.

Not only do we bargain with our spouses, we sometimes bargain with God. The risk in this, however, is that when the marriage continues to deteriorate, we may blame Him. We may transfer our feelings of anger and rejection from our spouse to our loving Father and withdraw from Him. While He is big enough to understand and forgive our anger, blaming God leaves us feeling we have no friend to go to for solace and strength. And this is a time when we need Him most!

DEPRESSION: "I WANT TO DIE."

Have you ever seen a baby cry so hard that she can hardly catch her breath? That's the way I cried during my divorce. I had never

wept that way before and haven't since. The depression was so excruciating that I contemplated taking my own life. Even though I wasn't
living an exemplary Christian life at the time, I knew these thoughts
were dangerous and not an acceptable choice. In the pit of despair
and too exhausted to pray, I would lean on the speaker of my stereo and
listen to worship music. The words of faith would flood my mind
with truth, and I'd begin to softly whisper praises to the loving One
who hadn't left me. Jesus alone sustained me; His compassion was
like no other.

Depression is a normal reaction to separation and divorce. You've
lost a spouse, the future you've dreamed of, and much more. It's
common for depression to manifest itself through lethargy, sadness,
anger, overeating, compulsive spending, drinking, and other destructive behaviors.

Do what you can to minimize the impact of depression on your
overall health. Try to get adequate rest, exercise, eat properly, and confide in a good friend. If you can, pray. If you can't, listen to worship
music or encouraging Christian messages about God's love.

While these things may not take away the pain, they may help
keep you from spiraling into deeper depression. However, see a doctor
or counselor immediately if you're having suicidal thoughts.

Ultimately, you are responsible for seeking help. God can heal
your hurt and renew your hope if you let Him.

Acceptance: "I'm Going to Survive."

I'm not certain when I fully accepted that my marriage was over. I
believe the acceptance came when I stopped wanting my ex-husband
to hurt as much as I was. Praying for the ability to forgive him and
others involved in the situation was instrumental in my healing. I no

longer viewed him as my enemy, and the need to get revenge or tell "my story" gradually ceased.

God encouraged me to be more forward thinking instead of dwelling on the past. He filled my mind with hope for the future. Eventually, I recognized and admitted my own faults in the marriage. And then the most amazing thing happened. With God's help, I was able to pray for my ex-husband's spiritual life and remarriage. I continue to pray for him to this day. Right now you may be wondering if it's even possible to arrive at this point. If you take baby steps toward healing and find a good support system, in six months from now I promise you will have a better outlook.

My heart will always bear a scar, but now the scar serves a higher calling. God took what evil intended to destroy me, and He used it for good. Now I point to my well-healed wound and say, "Look at someone who has survived and is thriving. I know what it's like to feel as though your whole world has ended. Let me help you find peace."

It's my sincere desire that within these pages you'll find comfort and rest for your weary soul.

Dear God,

You know what rejection feels like. You were deserted and despised by those You loved. It is a comfort to know You understand my pain. Please help me to recognize that I need to grieve many losses. Help me to walk through each one with the confidence that You are with me and will never abandon me.

Lord, I can't seem to find peace anywhere. I desperately need Your help. If I'm in denial, please reveal truth. When I'm angry, help me to give that rage to You. Replace those annoying thoughts with Your serenity.

Lord, one of my greatest needs is hope. Please give me confidence that my life is in Your hands and that even when difficulties come, I'm safe if I'm holding on to You. You are my anchor. You alone can bring me through this trial. I cling to the truth that You will never leave me nor forsake me. Amen.

(Portions of this prayer are taken from Deuteronomy 31:8.)

CHAPTER 1 QUESTIONS

1. What happens when we try to rush our healing after separation or divorce?

2. After a severe loss, what is the relationship between allowing your body and mind to grieve … and healing? What positive step(s) will you take this week to process your losses in a healthy way?

3. As you read the stages of grief, which one(s) did you particularly identify with? Why?

4. In what ways has anger affected your relationship with others? With whom are you angriest right now? Why?

5. Are you wearing your wedding ring? And if so, is that because you cannot face reality or because there is still hope for reconciliation?

6. How can a spouse know when it's impossible to save his or her marriage and time to accept the inevitable?

7. The author wrote that God filled her mind "with hope for the future." What is hope? Where can we find it?

8. How might praying a prayer like the one at the end of this chapter help to make a difference in a person's life?

To Do This Week ...

- Write down your stages of loss, and take one little step toward understanding and believing that the feelings are normal. Don't pressure yourself to move through the grief faster than is healthy.
- Find a divorce-recovery support group immediately.

2

When Do I Get
My Life Back?

TYPES OF LOSS

I am not afraid of storms, for I am learning how to sail my ship.
LOUISA MAY ALCOTT

I've read that divorce is worse than death—and I believe it—because it's a chosen abandonment. Along with the losses that occur with the death of a spouse—companionship, dreams, hopes, and financial stability—throw in rejection, humiliation, the battle over possessions and child custody, and the loss of friends and in-laws.

Divorce doesn't come with a handbook on how to handle the many big and little losses that accompany it. Who gets the house? Who loses it? Who pays the bills? Who gets the kids on weekends? Who keeps the married friends? What happens to relationships with in-laws? What about the pets?

The person who has been in an abusive or manipulative marriage may feel emancipation instead of sadness. He or she might be relieved that the stress and fear are gone, and often a sense of guilt replaces weeping. However, this person also needs to grieve the demise of the marriage covenant and the dream of what the family could have been. If those emotions are stifled and stuffed inside, they will rear their ugly heads in other areas of life and in future relationships.

If addiction has caused the collapse of the marriage, rejection is still present. Typically the addicted spouse doesn't want the marriage to end, but he or she refuses to get the help needed to overcome the obsession. This communicates to the nonaddicted spouse where he or she fits in the line of priorities. When forced to choose, the addict's true love affair is revealed. That person will cling to the beloved bottle or drug rather than the husband or wife.

In the following questions, you may recognize losses you're experiencing. I hope the responses will help you to navigate your own situation.

Loss of Friendship

My husband of seven years recently told me he wants out of our marriage and has filed for a divorce. I had no idea he was unhappy, and I'm devastated. He tells me we can still remain friends. Is that possible?

To ease the transition and guilt, many times one spouse will suggest remaining friends, but this is unrealistic. A friend is someone you can trust and confide in, share personal and confidential information with, call on in a crisis, and enjoy spending time with.

When spouses go through a divorce, they are no longer allies. Often one person can't and shouldn't be trusted. The offer to remain friends typically comes from the person wanting out of the relationship. It could be your husband's means of trying to soften the blow of rejection.

You must guard your heart and see things as they really are, not as you'd like them to be. If not, your heart will feel like a yo-yo, bouncing up and down, never fully moving through the stages of loss.

This doesn't imply a right to become bitter, spiteful, or obnoxious toward your husband. It also doesn't mean you shouldn't keep yourself open to marital reconciliation. If you have children, your goal should be to have a relationship where you both desire to communicate and work toward what's best for the kids.

But those things aren't friendship. Friendship assumes a tender, trusting relationship you and your husband no longer have. You need to move emotionally toward a place where your heart isn't vulnerable to your spouse's poor choices, and yet remain in prayer for the marriage to be restored. It isn't easy, and it takes time and the support of people who fully understand this complex situation.

LOSS OF "THAT PERSON I MARRIED"

I just had another huge fight with my soon-to-be ex-wife. The divorce is her idea. Her screaming, demanding, and threatening behavior is that of a complete lunatic. She is a totally different person from the one I married. What happened?

Divorce. That's what happened. Many people going through separation vividly remember a "Who are you?" moment with their ex. It could be that:

- You've denied the truth. This is her true personality, and until now you chose to ignore or minimize the severity of it.
- She's angry that her decision to leave the marriage has unpleasant consequences.
- She's using drugs or alcohol.

Whatever the cause, you need to seek help from a professional counselor or pastor to understand and cope with her responses.

Loss of Self-Worth

Since my husband left me, I feel ugly, old, and useless. I cry every time I look in the mirror because everything seems so hopeless. Will these feelings ever go away?

Many people describe divorce as a black hole into which they keep sinking. They can't find a way out of the abyss, and attempts to escape only produce more exhaustion. The loneliness that accompanies this crisis is very real and profound. It shouldn't be minimized.

At one time you felt valued and cherished by your spouse. Now you feel deserted and worthless. But your value isn't based on what your ex-spouse or others think of you, but on what God paid for you. He thought enough of you to pay the highest price possible to redeem you—giving the life of His own Son, Jesus. This is how much He loves and treasures you. This is the extent to which He will go to say, "You are precious to me. You are honored, and I love you" (Isa. 43:4 NLT).

Cling to this truth when all hope seems gone and when you don't feel lovable. Allow God to woo your heart with His tender compassion. From my own experience, I say assuredly, He won't ever abandon you. In fact, He says so Himself: "Never will I leave you; never will I forsake you" (Heb. 13:5).

Knowing this, take some practical steps to brighten your circumstances and outlook. A facial, new hairstyle or hair color, new clothes, or a new hobby can often lift the spirits. Join a divorce-support group and make new friends.

Loss of Self-Worth

When I lie in bed at night, I envision my husband and his girlfriend having sex. To understand why he chose her over me, I foolishly asked him what makes her more desirable—and he told me. How can I get these images out of my head?

In our quest to understand why, we often learn more than is wise for us to know. Most men and women in your situation have this problem even if they don't ask for details. They picture their spouses in the arms of the lover and replay their ex's treacherous infidelity like a video they can't eject from their minds.

Your mind will start to haunt you with whispers. *No one will ever love me again. I'll be lonely the rest of my life. Who could blame him for walking out? I'm boring, ugly, and fat. It's no wonder he left me for a beautiful girlfriend. She's much better in bed. That's why he wants her and not me.*

I only know one way to stop those thoughts. You must replace the images with the truth of God's Word. Only in God Himself can we find the ammunition and authoritative truth to battle those destructive images. You'll find a great resource to help you battle negative thoughts in Beth Moore's *Praying God's Word.*[1]

Loss of Emotional Stability

Since my wife has left me, I don't see any reason to live. Lately thoughts of taking my own life seem like the only way to stop the pain. I don't know what to do.

Crying became a daily routine, and when the racking sobs became more than I could bear, I thought about taking my own life. Numerous people going though separation have shared with me that while driving, they envision themselves intentionally swerving in front of an oncoming truck or into an abutment. These thoughts are typical for anyone who has suffered a severe loss. Our mind screams for the pain to end, and in the pit of despair, suicide seems like the only way out.

The warning should be when you consider planning a way to make these thoughts become reality. You need accountability. A doctor, pastor, counselor, close friend, or a suicide hotline can help if you are entertaining these thoughts more frequently. These people will teach you how to replace those destructive ideas with healthy ones. You might possibly need a temporary dosage of anti-depression medication.

God is the giver of life. We are not God; taking our lives is not up to us. It doesn't seem like it now, but God can heal your hurt and renew your hope if you let Him.

Loss of Child's Parent

My wife of nine years left my children and me for another man. I realize I haven't been the greatest husband, but this guy is no prize. How can a mother leave her children?

When the lure of forbidden fruit takes hold of a person's mind and heart, he or she often makes foolish choices. Your wife has been deceived into believing another man can make her happy, but the contentment she seeks won't be found in another man's arms.

When a mother abandons her children, the impact on their emotions, security, and self-worth is tremendous. Scripture describes it as the ultimate abandonment. "Can a mother forget the baby at her breast and have no compassion on the child she has borne? Though she may forget, I will not forget you!" (Isa. 49:15). Your kids desperately need to know you won't desert them too. The best thing you can do for them is to become emotionally stable. This will take hard work and prayer, but you can do it. A capable support group can provide the necessary environment for you to safely unload your hurt, anger, fear, and frustrations.

Also, seek help from family or church friends. Do you know a mature woman at church who would be willing to nurture your kids while you are at work? Do you know of a program for children of divorce in your community? Can you count on a reliable family to periodically welcome some extra kids to give you a few hours or a weekend of respite? Make your needs known. Often, people are more than willing to help fill the gap of love in your children's hearts.

LOSS OF FAMILY

My wife left me for another man. My in-laws have been very kind to me, and they are angry with her. She is furious that they are taking my side. Although I'm grateful for their support, I'm not certain what type of relationship I should have with her family. I don't want to lose them too.

As a kid, the saying "Blood is thicker than water" didn't make sense to me, but now I understand it. As angry as your in-laws are now with your wife, the bottom line is that she is still their daughter. In most cases, parents eventually gravitate back to their own child.

If you have children, keep the communication flowing smoothly with your in-laws and allow them to see their grandchildren as often as possible. But to guard your own heart, I suggest you gradually increase your emotional distance. A support group is an excellent choice to replace the encouragement and strength you found in your former spouse's family. Taking this action will prevent you from being hurt when your in-laws' anger toward their daughter subsides and their natural inclination toward her resumes.

The relationship I have with my ex in-laws is friendly, but we are no longer close. I pray for and care about them, and I occasionally send a card when appropriate. But we don't have the same cozy relationship we had when I was married to their son.

Loss of Belongings

When my wife of seventeen years told me she wanted a divorce, I was devastated. In order to keep a sense of normalcy for everyone, I left the home. My ex-wife and kids have the cars, furniture, dog—even my tool shed. They have everything, and I have nothing. This doesn't seem fair.

You're right: Divorce is rarely fair. I believe you did the right thing by allowing your children to suffer as little change as possible. Your willingness to allow them to remain in a familiar setting is wise. You understand their needs and unselfishly placed them before your own. Someday, when your children are old enough to recognize the sacrifices you made, they will thank you for it.

It's normal to resent relinquishing the sights, sounds, and smells of your home. Losing a spouse is hard enough, but leaving behind everything that is familiar makes the transition harder.

Creating a new home for yourself will seem awkward at first. Find a house or apartment that you can customize to your liking and fill it with things that will help you feel "at home." Let friends or family help you. In time, your new home will evolve into a welcoming, safe haven where you and your children create new memories.

Try to focus on what you do have. When I'm feeling defeated, I write a list of things I'm thankful for, such as a loving church family, good health, and faithful friends.

Loss of Connectedness

My married friends keep inviting me to dinner and other social engagements, but I can't seem to make myself attend them. I put makeup on and even get dressed, but then these anxious feelings take over and I feel paralyzed. My ex-husband and I have been friends with these people for more than thirty years—I don't understand why I feel the way I do.

You're experiencing the "third wheel" syndrome. You used to be married, as they still are, but now you are single. A feeling of disconnectedness from old friends is normal. And depending on the direction of the conversation, you may fear that you don't fit in anymore. Your life has drastically changed, and theirs has stayed the same.

Here are two things you can do. First, invite the women from the group to your home for lunch or coffee. This will provide an environment where you feel safe and sheltered. Tell them you appreciate the invitation to join them for dinner and that you sincerely desire their company. Explain that dinner with the couples is a painful reminder of your loss but that you would like to explore fun ways you can continue to socialize together as women.

Be prepared and guard your heart. Not everyone understands the grieving process. Don't take it personally if some friends think you are acting foolishly and decide not to participate. Gravitate toward the ones who recognize your situation and desire to help you heal.

Second, seek out other single women in the same situation. If your church doesn't provide opportunities to meet these women, research other churches that might. Tremendous healing occurs when we come alongside another person who has been in our situation. The greatest surprise will most likely come when God uses your pain to help another woman who is also hurting.

Loss of Church Family (or Community)

My ex-husband and I worked in full-time ministry. When he left our marriage, I also lost my church family and support system. Sundays are torture for me because everything in my life revolved around church activities. What can I do?

At one of my divorce-recovery seminars, two former pastors' wives shared their stories. In each case, they had lost much more than a marriage. The place that once provided a sanctuary of holiness now was an excruciating reminder of their husbands' unfaithfulness. Embarrassment kept them from attending their home church, so they began visiting large churches that offered anonymity, but they lost the comfort and support they so desperately needed. Their stories were heartbreaking!

You need a spiritual community. If going back to your former church isn't an option, look for another church that offers a divorce-recovery or grief ministry.

Other than a support group, I don't recommend you get overly involved in church activity or serve on committees for a while. Relax and let the body of Christ minister to you for a change. This is your season to heal.

LOSS OF HELPMATE

Shortly after my breast cancer diagnosis, my husband left me. Now I've lost my spouse and my breast. Although I'm receiving treatment, sometimes I'm not sure how to go on with my life. Whatever happened to the "in sickness and in health" vow?

Undergoing a divorce is devastating enough, but to cope with a life-threatening illness at the same time is beyond comprehension. I'm sure your oncologist has offered information about cancer support groups, and I suggest DivorceCare (see the resources section at the end of this book) to help you with separation issues. What I'd like to address here is your vows question.

I know a woman who, in her late twenties and pregnant with her third child, had a brain aneurysm that paralyzed her left side. Two months later, her father died unexpectedly, and the distress caused her to miscarry the baby. Her husband worked full time in a factory and took care of their other two small children. I've wondered, *How did their marriage survive all this loss?* Recently they celebrated their fortieth wedding anniversary.

Our society has had a major shift in its view of marriage and vows. This couple lived in a culture that focused on responsibilities more than rights. Today, society teaches personal rights over personal responsibility. This self-centered mentality produces the belief that bailing out on commitment as soon as the road gets rough is acceptable. When people with this mindset don't get what they feel entitled to receive, they believe it's their right to walk away. This dangerous, destructive attitude permeates our culture and is being taught to the next generation.

I would guess your husband is self-centered and has decided he has a "right" to a healthy wife. However, it's also possible he's afraid and needs help in understanding your condition. Only you would know, based on the past history of the marriage.

With a fear of sounding trite, I share with you that God sees the depth of your sorrow. He knows your needs and is capable of providing for every one of them. Women who have witnessed this truth firsthand can help strengthen your faith and assist you through your recovery.

I strongly recommend you ask your doctor and church for a support system to help you.

Loss of Health

I've always been a healthy person, but since my wife left I get severe headaches and I can't concentrate. I'm having a hard time sleeping, and my stomach feels like it's churning in a meat grinder. What's happening?

The physical effects of loss are unique to each person. During my divorce, I wanted to sleep all the time. It was a form of escaping. Often, I was so exhausted while running errands that I'd need to take a break and rest in my car.

Your body is reacting to the emotional stress common during a divorce. See a doctor to evaluate your symptoms. Many times medications can help.

LOSS OF IDENTITY

Since my divorce, I feel I no longer have an identity. Now that I'm no longer a wife, I don't know where I belong.

One of the most surprising losses during divorce is one's identity. A military wife shared with me, "My husband was an Air Force officer, pilot, and later a squadron commander. I was expected to be involved in military social activities and to support my husband. It was not mandatory, but it was understood. This situation created an identity that was ripped from me when my ex-husband decided he no longer wanted to be married. Who am I now? Not Mrs. Colonel So-and-So, not the squadron commander's spouse, not the Officers' Wives' Club member."

Although I didn't have a prestigious position, when the divorce hit I too wondered, *Who am I?* Then one day my pastor asked, "Is the divorce causing you to ask yourself, 'Who am I now?'" And somewhere deep inside, I found the words to respond. "Yes, I'm searching to know who I am, but fortunately I *do* know *whose* I am."

Dear God,

The sorrow and devastation of this divorce have stripped my mind of constructive thinking. I need tranquility where chaos now exists. Help me to know that I'm deeply loved by You, even if I don't feel it. I surrender every stage of this process to You. Help me to walk through these stages as You would have me. Bring me out on the other side of all this with a stronger sense of who You are. I need help to believe that there is hope for my children and me, and that You will never leave us.

Your holy and faithful Word says I'm not to fear, for You have redeemed me and I'm Yours. Help me believe that I'm precious to You and that You love me.

Lord, Your Word says those who look to You are radiant; their faces are never covered with shame. I don't feel radiant—I only feel lonely, humiliated, and discarded. I choose to believe Your Word when it says You are with me and are mighty to save me. Right now my emotions are fighting this truth. I want to trust Your Word when it says that You take great delight in me and will quiet me with Your love.

Lord, I'm overwhelmed with sorrow. I've never been so broken, but I'm going to lean on You because Your Word says You heal the brokenhearted and bind up their wounds. My shattered heart needs Your mending, my mind cries out for soothing silence, and my soul craves peace. Only You can provide these gifts. Remove the lies the enemy would use to destroy me and replace them with Your holy goodness. Amen.

(Portions of this prayer are taken from Isaiah 43:1, 4; Psalm 34:5; Zephaniah 3:17; Psalm 147:3; Isaiah 61:1–4; and John 8:44.)

Chapter 2 Questions

1. Some people believe that divorce is worse than death. What do you think?

2. What significant losses occur as a result of separation/divorce? Which losses have hurt you most? What can you learn through those losses?

3. Why should a spouse who has been in an abusive or manipulative marriage still take time to grieve and process emotions after the marriage ends?

4. Why is it hard for two spouses getting a divorce to remain friends? And how does friendship fit into the picture if children are involved?

5. Where does a spouse's lasting sense of personal worth and value come from during or after a divorce? What happens if we have primarily depended on our spouses to give us our value?

6. According to Hebrews 13:5, God will never leave us, never abandon us. What does this truth mean to you?

7. When is it better to know less about a spouse's or ex-spouse's wrongdoing and not press to learn more details?

8. According to the author, what are some steps a single dad or mom can take to help his or her children deal with separation or divorce?

9. After separation or divorce, what often happens between the spouse and his or her in-laws? Why?

10. What impact can making a list of things we are thankful for have on our attitudes?

11. The author wrote, "You need a spiritual community." What kind of benefits can such a community provide? Have you found community with others during this time? Who are they? How does a separated or divorced person find such a community?

To Do This Week ...

- Take a moment and think about someone else who has suffered a loss recently. Do something nice for that person. It doesn't need to be large: a flower, card, colorful gift, or piece of chocolate will do.
- Write a list of "praises": "Thank You, God, that I'm healthy, that I have a job, that my kids are healthy, that my family lives nearby and is offering to help, that I have a church that is supporting me, that I have food in the pantry ...

3

Barbie and Ken
Get a Divorce

CHILDREN

There are only two lasting things we can give our children.
One is roots, the other, wings.

AUTHOR UNKNOWN

On February 14, 2003, the *Atlanta Journal Constitution* reported, "After 43 years the legendary pieces of plastic have called it quits. 'Barbie and Ken have drifted apart,' said Russell Arons, vice president of marketing at Mattel. 'There are a lot of successful career women out there who don't want to get tied down,' Arons added. Barbie, born in 1959, will reclaim her identity as the California girl with a 'carefree and independent look.'"[1]

What does Barbie and Ken's divorce say to children about marriage? I think it communicates that when you get bored with your mate, you can just leave.

In the early 1970s, our society believed divorce didn't have much of an effect on children. But Judith Wallerstein's twenty-five-year study on divorce and children reveals the opposite. In her book *The Unexpected Legacy of Divorce*, she reports that a child's life is profoundly altered by the divorce experience.[2]

I know from experience how divorce can affect kids. When my parents divorced, I was eight years old. I have no memory of the day my mother, brother, and I moved away, except one brief flashback. I was walking down the stairs and thought, *I'll never be here again.* The following nine months are also a blur. I don't remember starting school or my new teacher. I have one vague recollection of a teacher praising my schoolwork, but I don't recall her name or face.

In contrast, I can remember the smallest details about the apartment we occupied before my parents' separation. I recall the gray swirled wallpaper in my bedroom and the green-and-white gingham dress my aunt Dorothy gave me for my birthday. I vividly remember my brother's crib, complete with teeth marks, and my treasured chalkboard where I would "teach" school to my dolls. The Tide box was stored on the bathroom windowsill, and our brown sofa was plaid. I remember being entertained by the white radio that sat on top of the refrigerator as I washed dishes.

Twenty-three years later, I found myself in my pastor's office, weeping. I'd been working for a boss who was impossible to please, and I finally quit. But instead of experiencing relief, I was overwhelmed with despair. When my pastor asked why I was so upset, I replied, "I don't know. All I know is that I feel eight years old again, and I can't do one thing right."

I was as perplexed as he was to hear those words come out of my mouth. Why had I said that? As the conversation unfolded, it became painfully clear that this little girl with memory loss believed she was the reason for her parents' divorce. The torture of that conviction had been too burdensome for my young mind to endure, so I forgot.

My memory of that season is still hazy, but now I know why. Don't let that happen to your children. Talk to them. Make certain that they understand that you and your spouse are not going to get back together ever again, if that's the truth. This truth is vital to their healing. Repeatedly affirm that they had nothing to do with the divorce. Mom and Dad made the decision, and the children aren't to blame. Help your children grasp the truth that they didn't cause the divorce nor could they have prevented it. When children are given vague "we just don't love each other anymore" answers, the chance of their internalizing and blaming themselves is much greater. Gary Sprague of Single Parent Family Ministry states, "The main reason why children of divorce think that it is their fault is because nobody has told them the real reasons for the divorce."[3]

Children can survive a divorce with minimal scars if parents are willing to do the hard work it takes to stabilize the home. This frequently means letting go of bitterness and anger that perpetuate a stressful atmosphere. Although both adults are responsible to help their children cope with losses, most of the work often falls on the custodial parent.

Seek God's guidance on how to create a home in which the children feel secure. Learn how to discipline properly and set boundaries. This demonstrates to children that they are safe and protected by someone who cares about them. Consider speaking with your child's teacher or school counselor. They may recognize depression or behavioral issues that you don't see at home. Often they are willing to become a significant part of the child's healing. And always remember, you may have divorced your spouse, but your kids didn't divorce their mom or dad.

Below are some of the questions newly single parents ask. For more information, I recommend Gary Richmond's book *Successful Single Parenting*.[4]

My wife and I just told our ten-year-old daughter that we're divorcing. She is very upset and sort of "zones out" when we try to discuss it. Why is she doing this?

Zoning out is her coping mechanism. When we don't want to hear something painful, we shut down. It's a form of denial.

She is at a tender age, so continue to try to communicate. Both parents need to spend a lot of time with her.

I also suggest you and your wife visit a counselor who specializes in children affected by divorce. He or she can advise you at what point her avoidance is abnormal. Have her see the specialist so she can begin to understand how to cope with the emotions and fears she is experiencing.

This isn't a quick process. Don't try to rush her. It will take patience and time.

I want to minimize the scars my divorce has left on our three young children. My ex-wife and I have a good relationship. We talk often, and I see the kids all the time. Are there other things I can do to relieve their pain?

Your children are fortunate. Divorced parents who communicate properly are admirable.

Here are a couple suggestions:

Help your kids buy a card or small gift for Mother's Day, their mom's birthday, and holidays. Your willingness to help your children communicates to them that they don't need to take sides.

Share special moments in your family's history. Show your kids pictures of earlier days when times were good. If possible, say something such as, "Grandma looked so pretty in her blue dress the day your mom and I got married," or "Your mom and I were so excited when we discovered she was going to have a baby, and that baby was you." It helps children to feel secure if they understand the family foundations and the truth that even in the womb, they were earnestly loved and desired.

My eleven-year-old son came home from soccer practice the other night and cried all evening. After much prodding, he finally told me that he was sad and angry that his dad doesn't come to his games or participate like the other dads. I've begged my ex-husband to attend, but he won't make the effort.

Unfortunately, you can't control the poor choices your ex-husband makes. What you can do is validate your son's feelings of rejection by using phrases such as, "I'm so sorry you are hurting. I know this is hard for you. I feel bad that your dad didn't show up." Don't minimize the pain he is experiencing.

Avoid the temptation to criticize his father. It might temporarily make you feel better, but it won't help your son. In fact it will attack his self-worth because when you criticize the father, children internalize those words as self-criticism. Address the behavior, not the person, by saying things like, "I know it hurts when your dad isn't there."

Ask God to touch your ex-husband's heart on this issue, and pray for a godly man to mentor your son. Ask your pastor or other church leaders if they know someone who might be interested. Many men would be willing to give their time if they knew of the need. If the man is married, make certain his wife is comfortable with his helping your son. For your own protection, keep your distance from the relationship between your son and his mentor. You might find it easy to become attracted to someone who treats your son with kindness. But be alert for any unwanted changes in your son's behavior. Sudden moodiness or a change in study habits could be attributed to your son's normal growth process, or it could be evidence of abuse. Keep the lines of communication with your son open and active.

To discredit me, my ex-wife tells our son terrible lies. She says I was physically abusive to her, that I don't pay child support, and that I don't really love him. I see my son weekly, as my visitation allows, but I'm distraught that he may believe her deception.

Kids see the truth. They aren't as gullible or naïve as we often think. And although they will protect a parent even in bad circumstances, they have radar that tells them something isn't right. Children tuck all the inconsistencies into their brains for future reference.

You can't change or control your ex-wife, but you can show your son your true character. Resist the temptation to criticize her and instead focus on your son's pain. Depending on his age, you could say, "I'm so sorry your mom told you that I don't love you. That must really hurt to hear those words. I truly do love you, (name). You are more precious to me than anything. And (name), you need to know that I never hit your mommy, and I do pay child support to help her raise you. If it would make you feel better to see the checks, you can ask me any time and I'll show them to you."

Use the child's name often. (A person loves to be called by his or her name.) Then reminisce about special times you've spent together. Make them real to him.

The absolute proof of your affection is revealed in making time for your son. Children spell love one way—T-I-M-E. Even when you don't see results, remain a godly, stable parent and don't give up.

My stepson Todd recently shared that he remembers his dad driving hours to attend his basketball games, even though Todd spent most of the time on the bench. His dad communicated unconditional love by caring enough to give Todd his most precious possession—time.

I also know of a dad whose daughter shunned him for many years because of the mother's lies. It took time for the child to see who was telling the truth, but the man and his daughter have a great relationship now. Eventually truth will win over the lies.

"So let's not get tired of doing what is good. At just the right time we will reap a harvest of blessing if we don't give up" (Gal. 6:9 NLT).

I am not receiving the child support that was decided upon in our divorce agreement. I've thought about prohibiting my ex-husband from seeing the children until he pays. Do you think this will work?

I realize this is a tempting solution, but I don't think it will accomplish what you desire. Children should never be used as pawns to control financial issues in a divorce. All legal, financial, or adult issues should be kept from children. They don't have the coping skills to handle such information.

Visitation and finances should always be two separate issues. I believe the only time a parent should keep a child from seeing the other parent is if he or she suspects the child may be endangered by the visit.

As frustrating as it is, the legal system is the proper channel to enforce child support. Fortunately, many states have instituted the removal of a driver's license or automatic payroll deduction to solve this problem.

God's view on neglecting your children is very clear. "If anyone does not provide for his relatives, and especially for his immediate family, he has denied the faith and is worse than an unbeliever" (1 Tim. 5:8).

When my children come home from visiting their dad, they are loaded with toys, gifts, and candy. I make a lower income than he does, and I can't compete with this extravagance. I look like the "mean mom" who disciplines, and he's the fun parent. How can I get him to stop?

You can't. You can explain to your former spouse how this is affecting the children, but be prepared if he won't listen. This "Disneyland dad" syndrome is an attempt to buy your children's affections. Often, but not always, this syndrome is motivated by guilt. This pattern of indulgence keeps children distracted from their emotional issues because it's easier to play than to discuss problems. Many dads don't want to act this way but simply fall into the pattern.

Your role is to be the most stable, available, dedicated single parent God enables you to be. If you are diligent, in time you will see results that will last long after the candy and toys are gone.

My four-year-old was fully potty trained before my husband left. Now he has started wetting his pants several times a day and has reverted to baby talk. I assumed he was too young to understand the divorce. What is happening?

Preschool children will often regress to infantile behavior during the separation. Your son is responding to the trauma of the loss of his daddy. Continue to reassure him that he is protected and that you won't leave him. Tell him that his daddy loves him. Discuss the problem with your ex-spouse and suggest that he spend more time with his son.

Do not talk baby talk to your son. Maintain as consistent a routine as possible. Providing a stable environment will help him feel safe.

My seven-year-old son has been in two fights this week at school. This never happened before his mother and I separated six months ago. He seemed fine when we first broke up, but now he's acting out. Why is he doing this?

Children will act out at school what they are feeling at home. When the anxiety and fear build on the inside, boys often release them through nasty words and pounding fists.

If he has experienced changes such as a new school, new home, loss of friends, and change in church, these will factor into his aggressive outbursts. Children don't know how to communicate their grief, so it shows up in unhealthy behavior.

Teach your child how to grieve. Ask him how he feels and then listen. Don't stifle the responses that make you feel uncomfortable or guilty. He needs to release them.

A peaceful home, parents who communicate with each other, and regular visitation with the noncustodial parent should help stabilize his behavior. If it doesn't, a counselor who specializes in children and divorce would be the next step.

My ex-wife got married recently. When my young daughter came for visitation, she enthusiastically shared details of the wedding, including, "And now I have two daddies." I yelled at

her that I'm her only father. She started to cry, and I felt horrible for lashing out at her, but I'm still fuming. What should I do?

Possibly her mom or new stepdad explained the marriage to her in this way. Regardless of why your daughter said it, she needs to feel totally comfortable sharing with you how she feels about the recent changes in her home. This is a huge adjustment for her. Your role is to create a tranquil atmosphere for your child, not an anxious one. If your daughter senses tension, anger, or hurt at the mention of her new family, she will avoid discussing it. Do you want her to stifle these emotions in an attempt to protect you, or are you willing to create an atmosphere in which she can tell you all that happens in her life—even the things you don't want to hear?

Apologize to your daughter and tell her you're not angry with her. Let her know that sometimes daddies make mistakes. Then tell her, "Now you have a daddy and a stepdaddy, and I want you to know that it's okay to like your stepdaddy. He is a nice man." If she wants to talk more about the situation, let her, but feel free to change the subject also.

Put your own feelings aside and attempt to establish healthy communication with her stepdad; this is the smartest response.

Seeing another person move into such a significant role in your child's life is difficult. I'm not saying you should ignore the emotions that come with your child having a new man living in her home. But take those feelings of fear or rejection to your support group, not to your child. Having a safe place to release the pain is key to making peace with the situation.

My wife left our three daughters and me a few years ago. The girls are in their teen years and want to date. I'm terrified because I know what their mother and I were doing at that age. I have a good relationship with the girls, but I feel so inadequate in this area of their lives.

Dad, take advantage of this prime opportunity. Take your daughters on dates and make certain it's fun! Show these precious ladies what to expect from a proper date.

In today's teen world, romance and chivalry have been replaced with raw sex and lewd behavior. To prove my point, take a stroll through the mall and observe the scantily dressed mannequins and models in advertisements. Give your daughters a vivid description of what a teenage boy has on his mind. Don't hold back, and explain what girls' clothing (or lack of it) does to a young man's hormones.

Talk about AIDS and other sexually transmitted diseases. If you aren't knowledgeable about these issues, research them on the Internet or contact a doctor. Get statistics about condoms, and clearly explain that they can't provide full protection from diseases. I know you're starting to squirm, but this is their future, and it can mean life or death.

You could also ask a young woman from your church to give your girls a female perspective. This should be someone they can relate to and respect.

Relax and have fun. View this as a time to create wonderful memories for you and your daughters. As your girls mature, they will thank you for it.

My thirteen-year-old son is beginning to inquire about sex. I've asked my ex-husband several times if he would please talk with him, but he refuses. I don't know what to do.

Most parents feel inadequate to talk to their children about "The birds and the bees." In a kind and non-condemning manner, help your ex to understand that this is normal. Then suggest a resource such as James Dobson's *Preparing for Adolescence.*[5]

If he still declines, then you are left with the task. Pray beforehand and use the material wisely. For questions you can't answer, seek wise Christian counsel from a family member or a trusted male friend in your church.

My children seem to enjoy spending time with my ex-husband's new young girlfriend more than they do with me. I feel that she's trying to take my place, and I don't like it. I don't know how to handle these jealous emotions.

If you haven't seen the movie *Stepmom*, I'd suggest you rent it. Although much of the movie, especially the ending, is unrealistic, the tension between the mother and the girlfriend is classic.

Let's review the facts. You are the mom, and for the well-being of your children you must be the disciplinarian. This isn't a fun job. No one likes it—especially the kids. You are the warden who makes them do their homework, take a shower, and eat their vegetables. The girlfriend, on the other hand, takes them to the video arcade (she must be really young to tolerate the noise), McDonald's, and the mall.

But where do your kids run when someone at school calls them ugly, humiliating names? Or when they fall off their bikes? Or when thunder and lightning frightens them? They want their mom. Mothers represent safety, comfort, acceptance, and unconditional love.

Several years ago I was in the hospital over Christmas. My mom had just moved from New York to Florida, but she flew back and surprised me at the hospital. I immediately started to cry when I saw her. There is a relief when Mom is there, even if we are adults. Somehow we know it's going to be all right when she's around.

No one can take your place. But you can harm your relationship with your children through jealousy. Ask God to help you rejoice that your kids are safe and that they get along well with this woman. Display to your children how pleased you are that she treats them well. Focus on the positive ways she's affecting them.

Three years ago my wife divorced me, and she has custody of our two children. I see my children fairly often, but I'd like to know how I could be more involved in their lives.

I congratulate you for not wallowing in self-pity. It appears that you understand how much your children need their dad. Don't ever underestimate the enormous role you play in building your children's self-worth.

There are many things you can do to stay involved in their lives. Here are a few suggestions.

- Consistently stay in touch. It can be as simple as e-mailing a joke or funny quote. But also send encouraging notes for them to save. Use e-mails, letters, faxes—any method available.

- Give them pictures of you doing a variety of things such as fishing with the guys, working, playing golf, sitting at the computer, or gardening. This makes them feel part of your life.

- Tell them stories about when you grew up, and if possible, show them pictures to put faces with your heritage.

- Discover your children's interests and talk about the things they like. Buy books on these topics or go to the library together to learn more.
- Pray for your children. Let them know you pray in all circumstances. Pray with them over the phone, e-mail, and in person. Express your thankfulness to God for them. Confirm what a blessing they are in your life and the lives of others.
- Praise them for who they are, not what they do. Instead of, "I'm proud that you play baseball really well," try saying, "Because you are my son, I'm always proud of you," or "You showed kindness and gentleness today toward that lonely girl at school. That is exactly what Jesus would do."
- Make sure they know how to reach you at all times.
- Look them in the eyes often and say, "I love you."

I am so exhausted when I get home from work that I don't seem to have any time or energy for my kids or myself. I feel guilty. What can I do?

This is the primary complaint expressed by single parents everywhere: "Help! I need more hours in the day." In the early stages of divorce a parent can feel so depressed that they have a hard time taking care of themselves, much less others. The key is to get information and assistance.

Books that specifically address the challenges of single parenting can help you in more detail, but here are a few popular tips.

- Take an objective look at your schedule. Are your children involved in too many activities? Are you?

- Don't be afraid to say no. Let someone else handle the car-pool, set up potluck suppers, serve on committees, or teach Sunday school for a while.
- Set goals and priorities. Chances are pretty good your kids won't remember the spotless kitchen floor or the karate lessons, but they will remember peaceful dinnertimes when they had an opportunity to share what happened at school.
- Give children chores. Robert G. Barnes wrote in his book *Single Parenting*, "Giving a child a chore is a valuable lesson for the child and an opportunity to promote family unity. The lesson taught to the child is one on how to accept responsibility."[6]
- Don't let guilt force you into society's mold of perfection. Things are different now that you're divorced—this year your house might not have a big garden or a fresh coat of paint.
- Ask for help. Friends and family can't help if they don't know your needs.

I'm so angry with my ex-husband that I can't stand the sight of him when he picks up the children for visitation. I don't know what to do to overcome this feeling.

Until you have accepted what is written in this chapter about the effect of divorce on children you will have a hard time overcoming this problem. You must determine in your heart that you will love your kids more than you despise your former spouse. This will require admitting and confessing that you are holding onto bitterness, and that it's harming your children.

People often say to me, "I would die for my kids." I respond, "I don't want to know if you will die for them, what I need to know is will you live for them? Because that's what they need."

Do you love your children enough to do what is best for them? If so, then read the chapter on forgiveness and follow the steps. If you are not ready to do that yet, then a temporary solution is to set up a neutral location with family or friends for him to pick up the kids.

Dear God,

I love my children more than anything. I'm terrified of the effect this divorce might have on them. I'm filled with fear, guilt, and anxiety. I need to remember that You are in control and that my job is to stay close to You. Help me, Lord, to be a godly example to my children even when I'm furious, hurt, or afraid. Please guide me on how to surrender those destructive thoughts and replace them with truth.

Lord, I need wisdom on how to be a single parent. It feels like all I do is scream and nag my children. I'm exhausted, and many times I want to give up. You alone can give me the strength, insight, and courage to accomplish this difficult task. I confess my need for You. I can't do this alone. Please bring others alongside me to alleviate the stress.

Lord, help me to forgive my ex-spouse for hurting the children. For the sake of my children and their emotional health, show me how to be kind even when I don't feel like it. Teach me, Jesus, what to do with the bitter and cruel words I want to say—that I feel I deserve to say. If I can't do it for You, then remind me,

Holy Spirit, that when I criticize the father/mother of my children, it deeply wounds my kids' self-worth and emotions. Give me the ability and willingness to keep silent when necessary.

Protect my children, Lord. Reveal any areas unknown to me where my children may be in emotional, physical, or spiritual danger. Teach me how to release the things I can't control, including how my ex-spouse relates to them or me. I can only improve my own relationship with the kids.

Provide for us, O God. You are the only One who can. I trust You. Help me to remember that You love these precious children even more than I do. Amen.

(Portions of this prayer are taken from John 14:27; Psalm 32:8; Ecclesiastes 4:9–10; Psalm 5:2; Mark 11:25; and 1 John 3:1.)

CHAPTER 3 QUESTIONS

1. If you have children, what are your greatest concerns related to how the divorce/separation is affecting them?
2. Why is it so important for parents involved in divorce to talk with their child about it? To explain that it's not the child's fault?
3. The author mentions the importance of doing the hard work it takes to stabilize the home after the divorce. What are some things parents can do to stabilize their homes so their children will have minimal scars?
4. Why is it important for one parent to avoid criticizing the other one in front of their children?
5. How does Galatians 6:9 relate to a divorce?

6. When a divorced couple with children can't communicate effectively about parenting issues, what should they do?

7. When should a parent keep a child from seeing the other parent? Why should visitation privileges be considered a separate issue from finances?

8. The author wrote, "Teach your child how to grieve." What's involved in doing this?

9. How can a parent who doesn't have custody of his or her children remain involved in their lives? Which of the author's ideas stood out? What other ideas might you add, based on your experiences?

10. Which tips might you add to the author's on how single parents can juggle so many responsibilities more effectively?

11. As you read the prayer at the end of this chapter, what did you think or feel? How might praying a prayer like this make a positive difference? Take time soon to look up the verses used in this prayer.

To Do This Week ...

- Write a note of love and affirmation to your kids and place it somewhere that will surprise them.
- Offer to baby-sit for another same-sex single parent.

4

God, Where Are You?

FAITH

I know God won't give me anything I can't handle.
I just wish he didn't trust me so much.

MOTHER TERESA

When my marriage died, it profoundly shook my faith. As a new Christian, I had assumed that since I had been faithful and followed God, He in return would bless our marriage. So why was He allowing this separation? Why wasn't He protecting me from divorce?

As a Christian, I believed God would automatically make sure nothing bad ever happened to my marriage. I didn't take into account that God gives us all free will. And if my husband decided to leave, God wasn't going to shackle him to the couch.

Although obeying God is always the best choice, I learned my obedience didn't guarantee a specific outcome for my marriage. I can't put God in a box and demand that He perform as I request.

Fortunately, I had great friends who stayed by my side while I struggled with God. For example, my friend Carol Young hugged me, cried with me, and listened to all my fears. Her Christlike behavior drew me back to God and helped restore my faith. I'm extremely grateful for her support during that horrible season of my life.

During my divorce, I couldn't find the energy or mental capacity to pray, so I would sit by the stereo and listen to praise music. The words to those songs became a "Mayday! Mayday!" type of prayer. On occasion, I could muster enough strength to open my Bible and let God soothe my heart. If your experience with God has been damaged or is limited, this is a terrific time to draw near to Him. Give Him your broken heart. He is masterful at binding up wounds, and He eagerly yearns for a deep relationship with you. Unlike people, He will never abandon or betray you. The security, gentleness, and love He longs to lavish on you will be like nothing you have ever experienced.

I've heard that God hates divorce. If that's true, why doesn't He stop my wife from leaving me? Why does she get to have a great time with no worries when she's the one who left the marriage, and I get stuck being miserable?

This is a version of humankind's oldest question: Why does God allow suffering? Why do the people who cause hurt seem to get off without any consequences? I don't claim to have all the answers, but I can tell you what I've witnessed over the years and what I know to be true.

People can appear to be blissfully enjoying the single life, but deep in their hearts, they may be lonely. I believe that when the "greener grass" starts to turn brown, they are left with a hollow spot in their soul. This side of heaven, you may never see the consequences of your ex-wife's choices. The key to surviving is to let go of that type of thinking and realize this is between God and her—it has nothing to do with you. God is your defender, and He is enough.

Try to focus on your own healing and not on how much fun your ex is having. I know that's much easier to say than to do, but you can do it. God hates divorce and knows your sorrow and your loss. Ask Him to heal your wounded heart. Jesus was rejected by those closest to Him—family, friends, and disciples turned on Him. He understands your pain and weeps with you.

I left my wife and children many years ago. I've become a Christian and would like to ask for my family's forgiveness, but I'm afraid. Is it too late?

It's never too late. I can't guarantee how your family will respond; it may take time for them to process the apology. The first phone call is the hardest. Pray before you contact them, and ask God to prepare and soften their hearts.

Express the depth of your remorse and assume responsibility for the long-term ramifications that your poor choices caused them. Explain that you don't expect them to forgive you instantly, but ask if they would be willing to consider it. Back off if the initial response is icy.

Your willingness to let them determine the pace of the relationship is vital. Any attempt by you to force, manipulate, or guilt them into embracing you is a clear indicator that you can't be trusted. If they need more time to digest the idea, then communicate with them in small increments. This could include sending letters that express your changed heart. When you are together, encourage them to share why they are angry, hurt, or fearful of trusting you. This won't be easy to hear, but it's necessary. With prayer and time, healing the relationship may be possible.

> **I haven't gone to church since I was a small child. Since my divorce, I'm so empty inside. I want to know more about God, but I'm afraid to go to church because of all the bad things I've done. What can I do?**

This is a perfect time for you to take the first step toward Christian community. Going to church for the first time might be intimidating. But in reality, imperfect people fill the church pews, and many of those people are also hurting. They aren't perfect, but they are learning and seeking forgiveness.

Although divorce is never God's will, He often uses it and other misfortunes to draw us into His loving arms. It's when we come to the end of ourselves that we seek the truth. If we haven't previously anchored ourselves to the One who never changes, this can feel very frightening. Fortunately, God is still on His throne and is passionately in love with you. He has provided Jesus as the way for you to be forgiven all those "bad things" you mentioned and be fully restored to Him. Listen to God's promise. "'You will seek me and find me when you seek me with all your heart. I will be found by you,' declares the LORD, 'and will bring you back from captivity'" (Jer. 29:13–14). You don't ever need to walk through life alone again. Jesus is the bridge between God and man. Because of His great love for you, He paid the price for all of your sins when He humbly died on the cross. God knew you could never be good enough to earn your way into heaven. Jesus is the only way to be reconciled to God. Now the choice is up to you to accept Him and what He has done for you. The Holy Spirit will help you to understand if you are truly seeking truth.

The night I accepted Christ, I wasn't really sure what the whole thing was about. But I prayed, "God, I don't fully understand what accepting Jesus as my Savior means, but I want to know truth. If Jesus is the truth, I'm willing to believe and give my life to You. I open my life to You." And God saw my heart. I wanted to believe. Understand, my friend, that even the ability to believe in God comes from Him.

If you would like to ask Jesus Christ to be your Savior and Lord, humble yourself and pray this prayer to God.

"Lord, I want to give my life to You. I'm a sinner, and I believe Jesus died on the cross to forgive my sins. I want to know Jesus Christ as my Savior and Lord of my life. Please come into my heart. Thank You for helping me to believe and understand this truth. Amen."

Never forget that all God seeks from His people is a sincere, repentant heart. He will teach you the rest. You will need to find a good church to help you grow. The DivorceCare Web site listed in the back of this book is a great way to find active churches in your area.

I was a very strong Christian when my marriage ended. But now I'm so mad at God for letting this happen to me that I can't even open my Bible. How can I get my faith back?

One of God's most astounding characteristics is that even the ability to have faith in Him comes from Him. Faith comes by hearing the Word of God (truth) and asking God to open our heart to that truth. (See Rom. 10:17.) We can't—and were never created to—do it "on our own."

Get alone with God and tell Him your thoughts. Be unreservedly honest. Scream, cry, yell, let it all out. God is big enough to handle your anger. Your rage won't shock Him—you're talking with the One who knows how many hairs you have on your head. He identifies with your agony and comprehends your pain.

Then give all of that betrayal, fear, fury, and sorrow over to God. Ask Him to transform your mind from one of anger toward Him to one that sees His compassion clearly. God weeps over your anguish because you are precious to Him. He wants you to be healed even more than you do.

My husband and I have decided to divorce because we aren't happy anymore. Some of my friends are saying this isn't a biblical reason to divorce. I find this hard to believe. Why wouldn't God want me to be happy?

Before I answer your question, I must first shed light on the word *happy*. Happiness is based on circumstances, and because theses continually change, it's impossible to be perpetually happy. When I'm buying a new pair of gorgeous shoes, I'm happy, but when I head out to my car and discover a new dent, my happiness quickly dissolves.

Joy, on the other hand, is a soul-deep, consoling peace and contentment. In our culture, we often pursue and even worship happiness, but what we're actually seeking is joy. Being happy is not wrong, but because happiness is temporary, it fails to satisfy.

You won't find anything in Scripture stating you can divorce because you are no longer happy with your spouse. Marriage is a lifelong covenant between two people and their Creator. Divorce might bring you temporary relief, but it won't bring the peace and joy you're seeking. It won't bring peace, because the marriage isn't the real problem. It feels like it is, because right now you dread the thought of staying married to your husband, but it isn't.

If you don't have peace and an abiding joy, it may be because you haven't fully been able to affirm the following:

- God will never leave me. (See John 14:18.)
- God has a wonderful future for me. (See Jer. 29:11–12.)
- God's ways are higher and wiser than my own. (See Isa. 55:8–9.)
- God cares about me. (See 1 Peter 5:7.)
- I'm precious to God and He loves me. (See Isa. 43:4.)

Your heavenly Father cares for you, and He has solutions for your unhappiness that reach far beyond your own reasoning. The power to live in obedience to God flows from having faith in His promises. God's assurance and pledge that He loves you will give you the desire to seek His ways above your own.

Pastors and churches have differing views on what constitutes biblical grounds for divorce. Unfortunately, many unhappy couples are told they have to "suck it up and hang in there." Based on Jesus' love, I don't believe God is a taskmaster shackling you to a marriage you hate. But I do believe He wants to make your marriage a living, thriving, and vibrant gift—even if you don't think that's possible. God desires to rekindle your heart with love for your spouse.

Even a marriage that appears dead can receive new life. God is famous for creating life out of nothing. Take a look at Adam. "The LORD God formed man from the dust of the ground and breathed into his nostrils the breath of life, and the man became a living being" (Gen. 2:7). He will do the same for your marriage. The question is, will you surrender and let Him? Will you trust that His love and His ways are better than your own?

If you are ready, pray this prayer.

"Dear God, I don't really want to restore my marriage. It feels cold, dead, and buried. I want it over. I'm tired of trying. I don't even like my spouse anymore, much less love him.

"God, I admit this is the first time I have considered that divorce might not be the best decision. The truth is, I'm afraid to trust You. I'm scared I'll get stuck living this way forever. Help me to believe you have my best interest at heart. Please transform my marriage. Please replace my heart of stone with a heart of flesh.[6] Show me how to be willing to have You change my heart.

"My knees are wobbly; I need faith and courage to seek reconciliation. I know I can't do this without You. I also know I can't change my husband's heart; You'll need to do that. My job is to ask You to change me, only me. Show me how to surrender my marriage and my whole life to You. Amen."

I'm not saying you'll fall back in love overnight. At times you'll feel like giving up. But God can restore your marriage—if you ask.

For three years, my entire prayer group prayed that my husband would come back to me. Recently he married another woman. With so many people praying, I can't understand why he didn't come back. Now I don't know if I should believe in prayer or God at all.

I believe God answers every prayer. I don't believe God answers every prayer in the way we request, however. Since God hates divorce, we can be certain that His desire would have been for your marriage to be reconciled. However, God has given us free will. If your spouse chooses to go against God's desires, God will let him. Are there consequences to those choices? Absolutely. But they are no longer your concern. Your ex-husband is married to another and is no longer available.

Now you need to refocus and adjust to the single life. Does your faith thrive only if God answers prayer the way you desire? Will you serve the Creator when He allows bad things to happen? This is our greatest challenge as Christians. The book of Job reveals one man's conclusion. "Though he slay me, yet will I hope in him" (Job 13:15). In other words, my circumstances don't change the way I view God's authority or faithfulness. He is worthy of my praise, even when darkness surrounds me. And because my Redeemer lives, He will provide a way out.

I keep searching for God in this dark valley called divorce, but I can't find Him. At the very time I need Him the most, He has abandoned me. Where did He go?

Be assured, beloved one, He hasn't left you. But sometimes when our grief becomes intense, it feels like He has. In times like this, we must trust what we knew in the light to still be true in the darkness. God is on His throne even when I'm in the pit. God continues to be omnipotent when I'm clueless. He is the same God who parted the Red Sea for Moses, and He is for me, not against me. (See Jer. 29:11–12.)

I don't believe God expects grief-stricken people to run around shouting, "Praise the Lord." Faking it through the pain just isn't His style. I base this belief on the psalms, in which we repeatedly see David groaning and crying out to God.

Surround yourself with people who understand this valley and yet have a strong relationship with God. Their presence and prayers for your life can carry you until you are stronger emotionally and spiritually.

I tolerated tremendous abuse from my ex-husband because I figured if I stayed with the marriage, eventually we would have a terrific testimony of God's restoration that would minister to others. Why didn't it work out?

Your motive was right, but your method was wrong. Tolerating abuse isn't love. It's actually the opposite of love to allow an abuser to continue destructive behavior.

When we love someone, we set healthy boundaries that allow the person to be responsible for his or her actions. By letting your husband continue to abuse you without consequences, you were helping to destroy the relationship. A strong marriage is built on trust, accountability, and unselfishness—not on enabling, manipulation, and control.

My ex-husband serves in a church-leadership role. During our separation, the pastor tried to make me feel welcome to stay, but it was obvious that my husband had "won custody" of the church in the proceedings. I'm not sure what I should do or if I even want to join another church.

It's a major mistake to isolate yourself while going through a divorce. A healthy Christian community that will assist you in the faith journey is crucial to the healing process.

Churches are like people: They each have a personality, strengths, and weaknesses. Searching for a new church can be time-consuming, but here are a few guidelines. Ask friends or co-workers for suggestions and review the worship and teaching style of each church. Check the Web sites of local churches and view the programs they offer.

When you have found a church that looks appealing, closely scrutinize its statement of faith for its core beliefs. Review any questions or issues you don't understand with a church leader.

Although doctrines differ from church to church, you want to be certain that there are no "gray areas" on critical issues such as Christ's deity, the Trinity, the virgin birth, salvation by faith, and the Bible being the true and inerrant Word of God.

I'm having a hard time going to church or looking at my Bible because of memories of my failed marriage. I had written in the margins of my Bible comments about my ex-spouse and our marriage. And the worship songs remind me of when we sang them together. What am I going to do?

This is why attending a support group is vital. I know a group of women who, during their divorces, set a time and place to meet every Sunday so they could sit together at church. This group has become their new family. Instead of dreading church, they grew to love spending time together in worship and fellowship. Buy the latest worship CDs and learn new songs. Use a new Bible that doesn't have your marriage notes in it. Don't turn to verses that remind you of your former husband. Instead, choose a book you haven't studied before. Ask God to rejuvenate the reading of His Word so that your soul is saturated with his love letters. Let this become a fresh breath from the Prince of Peace to you, His beloved bride.

I now realize I placed my husband before God in my life. I worshipped him instead of giving my heart to God. How could I have been so foolish?

If I had a dollar for every person who has said that to me, I'd be a wealthy woman. It's easy to idolize people, places, or things because they are more tangible than an almighty God who isn't visible. Our hearts are easily enticed by false idols. Discipline in God's Word and time in prayer are the tools necessary to alert us of the temptation to put people and things into a place they were never designed to be.

Loving and honoring our spouse is enjoyable, wonderful, and God-ordained. But when that love turns into worship or possessiveness, the relationship is in danger.

Our Creator knows that good things such as our spouse, our family, a job, food, or sex can easily become idols. Because God passionately loves His people, He cautions us to be alert to anything that may take His place and become a false god. We should never forget the high price Jesus paid for us. He alone deserves our devotion.

You're wise to have recognized the error of allowing your ex-spouse to become a god in your life. Now that you know this is an area of weakness for you, you can guard against it happening again should you decide to remarry.

Heavenly Father,

I never thought the day would come where I would feel so far away from You. And yet at the same time, I've never needed You as much as I do now. God, I need to know You are hearing my prayers. I need to know You haven't left me. I cry out to You as

David did so often in Psalms. Please come and rescue me from this pain. I'm more desperate for You than I have ever been.

Holy Spirit, I seek You. Please take my prayers to the throne of God. I'm so weak and weary that I don't even know how to pray.

Lord, Your Word says that I can lay all my anxiety down because You care for me and won't leave me. Help me, God, because I feel so alone. The very person I thought would stay by my side until death is gone. But You tell me not to fear, for You are with me. You declare that You are my God, You will strengthen me, You will help me, You alone will lift me up out of this pit of despair. Don't let this situation draw me away from You and into sinful choices.

God, please give me Your knowledge in every decision I must make during this divorce. Your Word tells me that if I ask, You will generously give wisdom. I need the mind of Christ. Please reveal the ways I can demonstrate Your love to my spouse. If there is any hope for restoring my marriage to the gift You created it to be, show me my role. Help me to forgive everyone involved, including myself. You are my strength. I will not be afraid. Amen.

(Portions of this prayer are taken from Romans 8:26; 1 Peter 5:7; John 14:18; Isaiah 41:10; James 1:5; and Psalm 27:1.)

CHAPTER 4 QUESTIONS

1. As a new Christian, the author believed God would bless her marriage and was shocked that He didn't protect her from divorce. What did she realize later?

2. What impact can Christian friends have on someone who is hurting and struggling with God?

3. How do we know that Jesus relates to our pain and will stand by us faithfully during the healing process?

4. In what ways do our views of God influence the extent to which we trust Him and draw closer to Him? Do you believe God is "big enough" to handle your emotions? Your pain? Why, or why not?

5. In what way(s) has your divorce/separation shaken your faith? Strengthened your faith?

6. Why, according to the author, is "accepting Christ" such a key step in developing a relationship with God?

7. Where does our faith in God come from?

8. When our emotions tell us that God has "abandoned" us, what can we do to remind ourselves that He is still with us?

9. Why is the willingness of a spouse to tolerate abuse in a marriage the opposite of love?

10. What came to mind as you read the Scripture-based prayer at the end of this chapter?

To Do This Week …

- Pray out loud, "God, I don't like this season of my life. But I'm going to trust You even if I don't feel like it. Please help me to believe that You can bring something good out of something bad. I need You, my kids need You, and I place this whole situation in Your hands."

- Go to a library, church bookstore, or Web site that offers resources for single parents and their children.

5

You Want Me to What?

Unforgiveness is like acid; it destroys the vessel in which it's stored.

AUTHOR UNKNOWN

FORGIVENESS

When I'm conducting a divorce-recovery workshop I can count on getting a laugh when I share that the "f" word during a divorce is *forgiveness*. People typically shun the subject during a divorce, going so far as to avoid a support group on the night this topic is up for discussion. That's because it's hard to fathom forgiving someone who has inflicted a soul-deep wound. An unwillingness to forgive is often based on a misunderstanding of the word.

Forgiveness doesn't mean pretending the offense didn't happen or was insignificant. The church has done a poor job explaining the difference between forgiveness and enabling. Many people assume that when you forgive it means the offending person should instantly be trusted or a relationship quickly resumed. That's incorrect and can be dangerous. It means you're willing to let go of the resentment and the desire to seek revenge. You give the offender and the circumstance over to God and lay them at the foot of the cross. You take your hands off and pray.

What happens if I refuse to forgive? Philip Yancey, in his book *What's So Amazing About Grace?*, says, "If we do not transcend nature, we remain bound to the people we cannot forgive, held in their vise grip. This principle applies even when one party is wholly innocent and the other wholly to blame, for the innocent party will bear the wound until he or she can find a way to release it—and forgiveness is the only way."[1]

The question isn't "Can I forgive?" but rather "Am I willing to let God teach me how to forgive?"

I only know one true way to encounter complete forgiveness: prayer. Jesus is the ultimate Forgiver; therefore, He can help us learn to forgive. Rejected and mocked throughout His entire ministry, Christ is familiar with betrayal.

Sometimes we see the rejection Jesus experienced as different from our loss. We wonder if He understands marital disloyalty. The book of Hosea makes it clear He does. "She's no longer my wife. I'm no longer her husband. Tell her to quit dressing like a whore, displaying her breasts for sale.... Wine has robbed my people of their understanding.... Longing after idols has made them foolish. They have played the prostitute, serving other gods and deserting their God" (Hos. 2:2 MSG; 4:11–12 NLT).

Can you hear God's grief? His fury? He laments, "Your declarations of love last no longer than morning mist and predawn dew.... Like Adam, you rejected the promise. You were unfaithful to me" (Hos. 6:4 MSG; 6:7 GW).

Guess whom God is referring to in these verses? That's right. We're the ones prostituting ourselves every time we choose to walk away from His love and protection.

Yet God is the author of forgiveness. Drink in the devotion and mercy He shows His people after their infidelity. "I will make you my wife forever; I will be honest and faithful to you. I will show you my love and compassion. I will be true to you, my wife. Then you will know the Lord" (Hos. 2:19–20 GW).

Finally, Jesus, while dying on the cross, uttered this prayer for all humankind: "Father, forgive them, for they do not know what they are doing" (Luke 23:34).

The ability to forgive comes from recognizing what it cost God to forgive me. Then I can stop comparing myself to my neighbor and measure myself against the holiness of God. Instantly, I recognize that I'll never repay His mercy. And when in humility I admit, "Yes, this person has sinned against me, but I, too, am a sinner," then I'm able to forgive.

RECONCILIATION

The very word *reconciliation* causes many separated couples to break out in a cold sweat. They panic at the thought of exposing their battered hearts to another potential beating. They're certain they can't face another rejection or betrayal. Sadly, few people are taught how to guard their heart and require trust to be re-earned when the covenant has been broken. They're so determined to avoid being vulnerable, they won't entertain thoughts of reconciliation. Yet, even marriages that have gradually decayed over many years can be restored.

Let me state clearly that I detest divorce; the devastation involved is heart-wrenching. I firmly believe it should be avoided if at all possible. I am totally committed to marital restoration and would dance a jig if a "going out of business" sign could be hung on my divorce-recovery ministry. However, the reality is that it takes two people to get married and only one to get divorced. And herein lies the problem.

For the person who wants the marriage to be restored, the most per-plexing question is, *How do I know when to accept the fact that my spouse does not want this marriage, and recognize this as reality in my life?* Most church leaders, parents, pastors, family members, and individuals seek a "formula" to answer this question. Unfortunately, a recipe for this doesn't exist because each situation is unique and should be addressed as such.

However, couples must take a few essential steps couples if recon-ciliation is to be successful.

First, both spouses must be 100 percent willing to do the hard work necessary to repair the marriage. The journey will be challenging, exasperating, and at times painful, but the results are worth it.

Second, if one or both spouses have had an intimate relationship (physical or emotional) with a third party, all communication with that person—phone calls, letters, e-mails, or visits—must end. If this other person works with the spouse, a job change should seriously be considered.

Third, both parties must be willing to go to counseling. The couple should take time to find the right Christian counselor, some-one who is qualified to deal with the issues, such as adultery, addiction, or abuse, that they're struggling with. Finding the right counselor is like buying a pair of shoes; sometimes you have to try on several before you find the right fit.

Fourth, restoring a marriage takes time. Rushing the process and avoiding or downplaying painful issues typically leads to another sep-aration and divorce. It's tragic when a marriage that could have been reconciled is destroyed because the root cause was never treated.

A marriage can't be restored if only one person wants reconcilia-tion, but that doesn't mean you should give up hope. Just because your spouse isn't willing to reconcile today doesn't mean he or she will never consider it. God understands how hard it is to pray life into a dead marriage. He will give you strength and wisdom and knowledge of what to pray. He will help you know when you should pursue reconciliation and when you should accept the marriage is irreconcilable. "Call to Me and I will answer you, and I will tell you great and mighty things, which you do not know" (Jer. 33:3 NASB).

My friends tell me I need to forgive my ex-husband, but I don't think I need to until he asks to be forgiven. He deserves to suffer for what he did to me. Why should I forgive him when he has never admitted he was wrong?

The book *What's So Amazing About Grace?* includes a perfect quote by Lewis Smedes:

> Vengeance is a passion to get even. It is a hot desire to give back as much pain as someone gave you.... The problem with revenge is that it never gets what it wants; it never evens the score. Fairness never comes. The chain reaction set off by every act of vengeance always takes its unhindered course. It ties both the injured and the injurer to an escalator of pain. Both are stuck on the escalator as long as parity is demanded, and the escalator never stops, never lets anyone off.[2]

Forgiveness isn't a fun process, but if you want to mend, it's vital. "For if you forgive men when they sin against you, your heavenly

Father will also forgive you. But if you do not forgive men their sins, your Father will not forgive your sins" (Matt. 6:14–15). Notice God says nothing about waiting until you feel like forgiving or that you only have to grant forgiveness if the person asks for it. God expects you to take the first step, beginning with a willing heart. The ability to pardon another person comes from God, not your own strength. He will help you. Your role is to surrender and to desire His way above your own. This may take time, especially if the offenses were severe. Walk toward forgiveness—the initial step is the hardest.

My husband says he'll move back home if I quit nagging him about the disgusting pornography Internet sites he visits. I think we need to be together for the stability of our kids, but I don't know if I can put up with that trash in our home.

I commend you for wanting your children's lives to be stable. However, restoration has to begin with your husband's commitment to surrender his sinful behavior. You can't make him give up this destructive activity with threats, nagging, or bribes. Until he craves freedom more than this prison of sexual addiction, you can't help him.

Protecting your children from damaging images is your primary responsibility. You can stand firm if you understand and are convinced of the serious consequences and long-term effects of pornography on children. The resources listed in the back of this book will help you with this difficult and ever-growing problem.

Pray to stay open to marital healing and for your husband to be released from this bondage. When he sincerely admits he is choosing addiction over his family, then repentance and restoration can begin.

Recently I left my husband because he is having sex with prostitutes. I found hotel receipts that trace his cheating back two years. He also has a long-standing pornography addiction. He says he loves me and doesn't want our marriage to end. My friends say that if he's repentant, I must go back to him, but I'm afraid. I don't know what to do.

In a noble attempt to preserve marriage, many family members, friends, and church leaders try to rush a separated couple into reuniting too quickly. However, until the toxic issues wreaking havoc in your home are resolved, reconciliation won't work.

You immediately need to visit with a Christian counselor whose expertise is sexual addiction. The counselor will help you understand your husband's destructive behavior and what your role should be in his—and your—recovery.

Judi Reid, advocate against pornography and sexual addiction, explained why you need help.

> He is caught in a vicious, escalating cycle that has the potential to mercilessly lure him into constantly seeking more frequent and more perverse sexual gratification than you could ever satisfy. This comes at the risk of losing everything, including his wife and family. You cannot fix him. You cannot cure him. He has to want to change.[3]

Pornography and sexual addiction are treacherous traps, and the work necessary to be delivered from them is multilayered. With excellent therapy, total commitment, and accountability, your husband can change if he earnestly desires to.

One major caution! It's extremely dangerous for you to renew a sexual relationship with your husband right now. He has exposed himself to sexual diseases that could kill you. I recommend you both see your physicians as soon as possible. In essence, he's having sex not only with these women but also with every person with whom they've had sex.

The other day my wife came home from work and said she's leaving me because she doesn't love me anymore. I'm stunned that my marriage might be over. I don't want it to end. What can I do?

I know this is a fierce blow, but do your best to calmly ask your wife to give you a more in-depth answer as to why she's leaving you.

Be careful about how you react to her rejection. Angry outbursts won't help you reconcile the marriage. Neither will self-pity, whining, clinging, begging, or threats of suicide. Getting even by dating or having an affair also won't work. Those behaviors communicate to your wife that she is off the hook. As an added bonus, they relieve her guilt because she then feels justified in leaving.

You can tell your wife that although you're deeply hurt, you're willing to learn from her where you may have failed the marriage. Ask for reconciliation, but recognize that she might not respond positively at first.

Explain why you believe there is hope for your marriage and the steps you're willing to take to improve the relationship. Share with your wife that you value the marriage so deeply you're willing to go to counseling. You can't force her to agree to reconciliation, but you can encourage the decision and you can pray.

One consideration: I've observed that people having an affair often ease their conscience by saying, "I don't love you anymore" or "I'm just not happy," rather than saying, "I'm leaving you for someone new." If your wife is having either an emotional or physical affair, you'll need to see a counselor.

My husband left, and I can't afford our huge house. My friends tell me to sell it, but I'm afraid that will destroy any chances of restoring our marriage. Won't selling the house communicate to my husband that I've given up?

It's normal to assume losing the home you shared will end any hope of restoring the marriage, but it's unfounded. View the sale as a good thing. If finances were an issue in the separation, then down-sizing might relieve one stress factor. Remember, reconciling doesn't mean going back to the way things were; it means starting fresh.

I had a yearlong affair. I've asked my wife to forgive me, but she says she can't ever trust me again. Is there a way to get my wife back?

The cliché "actions speak louder than words" is true. Words aren't enough to prove your repentance. If your marriage is to have any hope, your wife will need to see over a period of time that you're a changed man.

Communicate your sincerity by doing the following:

- Get counseling even if she won't go with you. Find out why you had an affair—it's crucial for healing.
- Get into a Christian men's accountability group.

- Read books that address men's issues, such as *The Man in the Mirror* by Patrick Morley.
- Practice humility. Don't demand, manipulate, or try to control your wife's actions or feelings.
- Admit that you've demonstrated that you're untrustworthy. Mention concrete ways—such as meeting with the pastor, giving her access to your e-mail, and not traveling alone—in which you're willing to be held accountable so that trust can be rebuilt. Let your wife make suggestions too.
- Pray for God to soften her heart.

If you do divorce, remain faithful to your marriage covenant and continue to pray for restoration. If your wife remarries, then there is nothing more you can do.

My husband had an affair and now says he's sorry and wants our marriage restored immediately. He says if I really want the marriage to work, I will never mention the affair again, and that sexual intimacy will restore our marriage. I'm still devastated over his betrayal. I don't know what to do.

Your husband's demanding attitude reflects a lack of true repentance. When a spouse has an affair, restoration has to begin with his repentance. Someone who recognizes the magnitude of his offense is remorseful, humble, and sorrowful. If your husband were repentant, he'd be willing to accept consequences and work to regain your trust and prove he has changed.

Repentance is the pivotal word in this situation. What does a truly repentant person look like? Let's use a different scenario to illustrate. Imagine my employer catches me stealing money. I'm sorry for the offense, I beg for a second chance, and he gives me one. Would you expect this employer to instantly trust me again with his bankbook or the combination to his safe? No, I would need to earn his trust again. Because of my poor choice, I must now demonstrate that I can be trusted. My dishonest behavior has put me in a position to prove, over a period of time, that I am sorry and can be honorable. To make urgent demands of my employer or become angry at his request is ludicrous.

When a person breaks the marriage covenant and then uses control or demands immediate restitution, this reveals his or her true heart. A person who comprehends the magnitude of his offense is remorseful, humble, and sorrowful. A repentant heart says things such as, "I know what I've done has made it hard for you to believe my words. I've destroyed the marriage vows, and my sinful choice has shattered your heart and dreams. I understand there are painful consequences to what I've done. I won't pressure you, but if you are willing to let me prove to you that I am truly sorry, I'll do whatever it takes."

King David in the Bible provides an excellent example of true repentance. Listen as he pleads with God after his sinful affair with Bathsheba.

> Wash me clean from my guilt. Purify me from my sin. For I recognize my rebellion; it haunts me day and night. Against you, and you alone, have I sinned; I have done what is evil in your sight.... But you desire honesty from the womb, so teaching me wisdom even there. Purify me from my sins, and I will be clean; wash me, and I will be whiter than snow. (Ps. 51:2–4, 6–7 NLT)

This was a guy who was sincerely sorry for what he had done. He realized his evil deeds had cost him dearly, and he begged God to restore him. He took full responsibility for his sinful choice. He didn't blame anyone else. When an affair has severed the marriage covenant, restoration begins with repentance.

Seek godly counsel from a marriage counselor who can help you show your spouse tough love. Your spouse also needs to be willing to get counseling—and a clean bill of health—before you restore sexual intimacy.

I took a passive role during the divorce, thinking that being passive equated "turning the other cheek." My hope was that if I didn't force my ex-wife to be responsible, she would be more likely to reconcile. As it turned out, I was engaging in fantasy thinking.

Leniency often appears to be merciful, but it isn't. Quite often, the behavior we interpret as loving actually causes further damage. How do we correct distorted thinking? Two books I recommend are *The Mind of Christ* by T. W. Hunt [4] and *Boundaries* by Henry Cloud and John Townsend. [5] They helped me understand how to obtain the mind of Christ and gave me the tools to replace my muddled thoughts with clear thinking. They explain how to think as God would and how to recognize the warning signs when our thinking gets confused or warped.

Dear God,

I know You yearn for my marriage to be restored. Your Word says You created marriage, and it is a good thing. I'm confused as to how I should feel. Please show me what role I've played in tearing the marriage down. Help me to see what my part should be in seeking restoration. Show me what to do.

When I want to scream at my mate, help me to remember that lashing out won't help the situation. Holy Spirit, speak through me and give me the ability to communicate clearly, calmly, and reasonably.

Your Word says You will fill me with peace as I believe in You. I desire the overflowing hope described in Your Word. Thank You, Holy Spirit, for bringing me this desperately needed optimism.

Heavenly Daddy, I need to learn how to forgive. On my own, I have no ability or desire. I look to You, Lord. I don't really want to forgive my spouse, but I believe Your Word and its commands. Help me understand that following Your way is a good and wise thing, because You yearn for me to be set free from bitterness.

If You reveal that the marriage is over, help me to accept this and allow You to rebuild my life. I know You have a future for me. Show me how to surrender my marriage and my whole life to You. Amen.

(Portions of this prayer are taken from Malachi 2:16; Genesis 2:23–24; Romans 15:13; and Jeremiah 29:11–12.)

CHAPTER 5 QUESTIONS

1. What are some of the reasons many separated couples are afraid to try to get back together?

2. What, according to the author, are four important steps a couple must take when trying to achieve successful reconciliation?

3. What's the difference between happiness and joy? Why is this difference important for both spouses to remember when their marriage is in trouble?

4. Where do we receive the power to obey God?

5. Why is pornography so damaging? How can a spouse know what kind of line to draw when the other spouse uses pornography?

6. If a spouse is having an affair, what should the other spouse do? Why is recovery from an affair often a lengthy process?

7. What is true repentance? What are some signs that a spouse is truly repentant?

8. How important a role does prayer play in forgiving a spouse? How does forgiving someone else benefit you?

9. Where do we get the ability to forgive? Or learn how to forgive?

10. Have you taken steps to forgive your spouse? Why, or why not? If not, what have you gained by refusing?

TO DO THIS WEEK ...

• Write out a note of forgiveness to someone involved in your circumstances. (For example, former spouse, family member, former in-laws, etc.) You do not need to mail it— and you may even want to destroy it—but write it anyway. Do you need to forgive the man or woman in the mirror?

• Look into some type of group exercise. Many churches offer classes or groups that walk together ... and it's free!

6

Where Are Those Pennies from Heaven?

FINANCES AND LEGAL ISSUES

God is your source, not people.

LARRY BURKETT

Money, money, money! During divorce, finances become the battle-ground for control, and all too often the war turns bloody. Income level doesn't determine which couples duke it out—whether the family is making four figures or six, the combat is similar because the real issue isn't cash.

People frequently use finances to manipulate, intimidate, and/or control others. When money is used as a vehicle for revenge, the offended party is really saying, "I'll make you pay and pay and pay again for hurting me." And the fight begins.

In my own situation, I panicked over finances. When I reflect back, I wonder why fear gripped me so severely. I'd lived on my own for years before getting married. I paid all my own bills and survived without any help. Why, during divorce, did my checkbook produce such trepidation? I've concluded it was just one more area where I felt out of control and betrayed. In marriage, I had relaxed about finances, and although I still worked, I depended on my husband to provide. Money was one more stinging reminder that I had been deserted.

Occasionally I'll meet someone recently separated who says, "I know my spouse and I won't fight about money. He has agreed to maintain all the monthly payments." I cringe because I know from experience that within a few months, the guilt-prompted promises will fade. When legal bills, mounting payments for two households, and the temptation to splurge on a new single lifestyle set in, these commitments will dissolve.

In his *Fresh Start Divorce Recovery Workbook*, Tom Whiteman says, "If finances were tight before a breakup, they will be suffocating afterwards."[1] And right he is!

Many people believe they can maintain the same standard of living after a divorce as they did when married. This unrealistic thinking compounds the disputes and problems. In reality, couples may need to downsize the home and car, buy cheaper clothes, cut out extras such as cable TV and manicures, eat out less often, and clip coupons. These are the sobering consequences of divorce.

The transition is particularly difficult for the stay-at-home mom who suddenly finds herself forced to enter workplace and leave her kids in daycare. This woman, often in a state of depression and rejection, desperately needs help from the church.

Professionals are out there who specialize in divorce and can help you understand what to expect in court. I recommend a mediator, family-law attorney, and divorce-certified financial planner. The obvious question is, "How do I find the best in these fields?" I suggest reading chapters 12–14 in legal expert Joseph Warren Kniskern's book *When the Vow Breaks*.[2]

Here are some observations from people who have experienced legal challenges in their divorces:

- "Don't assume a lawyer is qualified just because he or she is a Christian."
- "Take a friend with you to the lawyer; it's almost impossible to concentrate and remember the crucial and necessary questions."
- "Don't listen to legal counsel from friends, coworkers, or family members. They aren't qualified attorneys. Their emotional involvement prevents them from giving sound advice."
- "My attorney was able to look five, ten, fifteen years into the future and plan safely for me while I was just trying to get through day-to-day stuff. Unfortunately, I paid the price for not listening to her."
- "I felt bullied by my lawyer; he wasn't willing to listen to what I wanted."
- "Even though I had to borrow money from my parents for the retainer, I got my own lawyer. It was a wise decision even though separate lawyers made the divorce process longer and more expensive."
- "I didn't want to fight, so I just gave up and let the attorneys decide. I ended up with nothing."
- "I wish I hadn't let my attorney rush me through the divorce so quickly."

Some legal experts are honest and excellent, and some aren't. Frequently a person divorcing has no prior experience in hiring an attorney. In addition, the stressful and complicated decision must be made at a time when concentration levels and decision-making skills are at an all-time low. I highly recommend taking your time to decide.

When seeking professional help, ask people you know and trust—preferably those who have been through a divorce or who work for a lawyer—to suggest an attorney. Occasionally a mediator can give a list of competent lawyers, but be cautious. The mediator and the attorney may work together and feed each other's pockets.

After you've found an attorney, set up an interview or consultation appointment. Take someone with you who isn't emotionally involved. This person may see and hear things you are incapable of noticing.

Many lawyers will provide a first visit free of charge. If he or she tells you everything you want to hear, it may mean that lawyer is willing to say anything to get your business. A good lawyer will tell you the truth, even if it hurts.

Finally, remember that God is our provider, not court systems, alimony payments, or a spouse. Sometimes He uses those things to provide, but not always. Therefore, seek His wisdom before you make legal and financial decisions. Ask for divine guidance in determining what financial settlement is fair and wise.

Your attorney may think you're foolish not to try to get everything you can financially. But God wants you to do what's right regardless of how you've been treated. Submitting to God brings Him glory. Philippians 2:3 (NASB) tells us, "Do nothing from selfishness or empty conceit, but with humility of mind let each of you regard one another as more important than himself." This verse is hard to put into practice, but God can and will give you the strength to do it.

God is the source for all our needs, and He will be faithful even if your spouse isn't. This doesn't mean you are to roll over and play dead or become a doormat, nor does it mean you're required to relinquish everything you own. What I'm recommending is that you seek God's will. God's ways are always higher than man's. This act of respect toward your spouse may be the very thing God will use to soften his or her hard heart.

I need to find a divorce attorney, but I don't know where to begin. Any suggestions?

Begin with references from people you trust. If you're involved in a divorce-recovery support group, ask members for suggestions. Do the research and ask divorced friends these questions:

- Did your attorney let you interview him before hiring?
- Does your lawyer specialize in family law? Does she spend at least 50 percent of her time focused on divorce issues?
- How many divorces does he handle per year?
- Did you feel she listened to your questions or concerns?
- Did your lawyer prepare for court adequately?
- Was the fee comparable to others?
- Did your attorney call you back within a reasonable time frame? Or did he delegate that to others?
- Did you get the impression that your attorney cares more about people than money?
- What's one thing you wish your attorney had told you?

My husband says we don't need two attorneys and that using his attorney will save us money. He promises not to cheat me and to offer a fair settlement. What do you suggest?

In the early stages of separation, couples often want to divorce as quickly and cheaply as possible. As time progresses, many become angry and vengeful. Therefore, I would never suggest signing a divorce agreement without at least one consultation with your own attorney. If you have no property, no children, and no debt, there's a slim possibility you could use one attorney—but those cases are rare.

My husband asked me for an uncontested divorce using his attorney. For eighteen years I've deferred to his judgment on all decisions, but this time I said no. I want my own attorney. He acts furious and hurt that I won't trust him and is accusing me of being vengeful, greedy, and un-Christian. He's the one walking out on our vows. Why am I the bad guy?

He isn't getting what he wants. He assumed you'd roll over and play dead. You didn't, so he's angry. He believed divorce would be easy, but realizes now it might cost him something, and he's not happy about that.

Do evaluate your motives. Are you being vengeful or greedy? Or are you simply protecting yourself and your future? If your intentions are pure, you'll eventually have peace of mind no matter what your husband accuses you of doing. It's neither selfish nor materialistic to get legal counsel. It's wise.

My wife wants a divorce and has seen an attorney. Friends and family tell me to get an attorney also, but I'm afraid my wife will think I've given up on the marriage if I do.

A consultation with an attorney will arm you with much-needed information should your wife pursue divorce. Keeping yourself in the dark won't help your marriage. It only makes you vulnerable to further problems.

I am not suggesting you flaunt a visit to an attorney in front of your wife or that you become nasty or unpleasant. Merely go and learn what your options are, where you stand financially, and what to do if she insists on ending the marriage. I'd continue to clearly state to her that you are opposed to the divorce, you love her, and you are willing to do what it will take to restore the marriage.

People often think seeing an attorney or attending a divorce-recovery class puts the final nail in the divorce coffin. I disagree. It's the person who is unprepared and shocked by the financial blow that has a hard time functioning afterward.

I've been out of the workforce for fifteen years as a stay-at-home mom. Since my husband left, I've begun looking for work. I'm shocked at how low the wages are, and I sense my skills are outdated. What am I to do?

First, don't panic; you can do this. Most communities have resources and support groups to help women reentering the workforce. You're not alone!

If your technology or computer skills are outdated or limited, research a local community college for courses offering the basics. Today almost any job will require some computer knowledge. Receiving training will help you feel more equipped for the job market, and it will educate you on computer "lingo" that can be intimidating. Be sure to check on school grants and low-interest loans.

Second, be prepared to take a lower paying job to get your foot in the door. An excellent work ethic, showing up on time, a reputation for honesty, and being a team player will speak volumes to a supervisor. Once your boss sees you have a positive outlook and willingness to learn new skills, you'll be seen as a valuable employee.

I need to reenter the workplace, but I'm not sure where to begin. I don't even know what I'm good at doing, and my self-worth is at an all-time low.

Try a career-assessment system, such as Crown Financial Ministries' Career Direct.[3] This tool will print an assessment based on your personality, skills, and interests. I like this system because it also helps you find a career based on your values. It will guide you toward the education or career that best suits you.

God has wired each one of us in a distinctive and unique way. He has created you to do something better than anyone else. You just need to find out what that is.

My ex-husband was in charge of taking care of all the bills. Now I'm alone and don't know where to begin.

The best place to start is with a budget. An efficient budgeting guide can show you the necessary categories and various expenses. You can get these from the library, Web sites, and bookstores. If you feel overwhelmed, ask your pastor if someone in the church with accounting or banking skills can help. If the recommended person is a married man, be sure to have a third party join you. If no one is available, contact Crown Financial Ministries to ask about their volunteer budget counselors.[4]

If you have past-due bills, call your creditors to review your accounts. When calling, have your most recent bill in front of you and be prepared to give the employee your account number. Explain your situation and don't feel embarrassed or ashamed. Companies frequently deal with this and would rather help you now than when you are several months in arrears.

I have a budget, and it shows I have enough income to cover my expenses, but I'm ending up with no money by the fourth week of the month. Why isn't my budget working?

I'll bet your missing money is hiding in the miscellaneous category. Most people are unaware of how much they spend every month on incidentals. Try this: For one month, journal every penny you spend. And I do mean every penny. This includes money for gum, coffee, a muffin, newspaper, lunch—all the small stuff. At the end of the month, add it up. You may be shocked to find what a budget buster you have hiding there.

If this isn't the problem, see a budget counselor. A fresh pair of eyes will help reveal a potential error.

My ex-wife wastes my child-support payments on frivolous stuff for herself, while my kids are eating macaroni and cheese every night for dinner and wearing worn-out clothes to school. I've considered stopping the payments and using that money to buy my children the things they need. Doesn't this seem the wise thing to do?

This might seem a logical solution, but it may not be a legal one. Is your ex-wife paying for their housing and utilities? Does she supply the children with basic toiletries such as toothpaste, Band-Aids, and cough medicine? If so, courts would determine she's providing for them.

A possible solution may be for you to evaluate the things she does provide and view your support as going toward those items. This doesn't imply she shouldn't be serving nutritious food or meeting the children's basic needs. But you must review what you can control and what you can't. Letting go of the things over which you have no control, even those that are hurting your children, is one of the most challenging issues in divorce.

I know many men who have paid for things that weren't addressed in the divorce agreement, such as dental braces, piano lessons, baseball camp, and speech therapy because they felt they were essential benefits for their kids. Whenever possible, try paying the provider directly for those kinds of things. It helps to avoid conflict.

I'm considering taking my husband back to court for more child support. How do I determine what's a fair amount?

First, ask yourself what your motive is for taking your ex back to court. If you need more money because your children are getting older, prices have risen, and their needs are greater, then it's a reasonable request. Evaluate your budget and show your ex-husband the areas where the kids' needs aren't being met. If he won't listen, then you may need to get legal help.

If your motive is one of anger, vengeance, or a desire to punish him, you need to seek God for His perspective. Don't listen to anyone who encourages you to "stick it to him, and make him pay." When a person is emotionally wounded, retaliation feels appropriate, but it won't bring peace.

My ex-wife continually comes to me with ridiculous requests for additional money. I pay her child support, but she wants more. This month she wanted me to buy my daughter a school jacket that cost $250. I didn't have the money, so I said no, and now my daughter won't speak to me.

The issue in this situation isn't financial—it's control. Many couples use money to manipulate one another. No one wins. And children suffer the most.

If possible, sit down with your ex-wife and find out what's prompting her desire for more money. Is it revenge? Or guilt that her children are living in a divorced situation? If communicating isn't an option, then you'll need to discern the reason for her behavior on your own.

Talk with your daughter and explain that your love for her isn't determined by what you buy her. Tell her how precious she is to you and remind her of fun times you share together. If she appears to ignore you, keep talking anyway. Remember, she may be hurt and angry over the family's breakup.

If she doesn't warm up to you, keep reaching out. If she won't speak to you in person, send letters or e-mail. The key is to stay involved. Go to her sporting events and concerts. Show her you care with more than words or gifts. Do it with actions. Make yourself available and pray for God to soften her heart.

I've paid my child support faithfully for two years. I've recently remarried and have a child on the way. I don't think I can continue to pay my ex-wife what we decided in the divorce agreement. Shouldn't the change in my circumstances determine how much I pay?

When a couple has children, they are making a guaranteed commitment to support those children. They did not ask to be brought into this world. You took on the responsibility to provide for them until they're adults. Your decision to remarry and take on additional financial burdens has no bearing on your responsibility to the children from your first marriage. It's your duty to continue supporting them.

My husband and I are divorcing, but my name is still on a joint credit card. He says it's not a problem and that he will pay the bill. Is this safe?

The sooner you can get your name off of joint credit cards, the better. Call the credit card company, explain the situation, and ask for the best solution. Every bank has a different system for handling joint accounts. Anything with your name on it requires you to shoulder financial responsibility if your spouse defaults. Money is frequently used by one ex-spouse to punish the other. The less opportunity for this to happen, the less stress you'll face. Get your own card.

An additional caution: When you sign for a loan or mortgage, you are responsible to repay until or unless the loan has been rewritten and/or refinanced without your name or signature.

I knew a woman who asked that her name be removed from a home equity loan in lieu of alimony. Her husband agreed, but the loan was never refinanced in his name alone. When he defaulted, the bank looked to her for payment. Her divorce agreement didn't protect her from being responsible to pay this money. While she had grounds to take her ex back to court, it cost her more in legal fees.

Her attorney should have explained the serious consequences of not getting her name removed from the loan. She believed that since her divorce papers released her, she couldn't be held legally responsible. She was misinformed.

When I became a Christian, I learned to tithe (give one-tenth of) my income. Since my spouse left, I'm afraid to continue giving. Does God expect me to tithe now that my finances have changed so drastically?

God isn't looking at the dollar amount as much as He is your heart. It's normal to be concerned, but ask yourself why fear has replaced trust. Do you rely on God? Do you see Him as being a faithful provider?

Ask God to reveal the root of your apprehension. Since your spouse has abandoned the marriage covenant, you may fear that your heavenly Father will also leave. God understands your anxiety, and He will reassure you with declarations of loyalty and devotion. You are His precious child and He won't desert you. What a promise!

After you've settled the trust issue, ask Him for guidance on financial giving. For a while you may need to give less. God doesn't use a calculator. He's far more concerned about your spiritual healing and ability to trust Him again than He is a specific dollar amount.

My husband made a good living, so we always had a large, lavish house. I don't feel my children should have to downsize just because their parents can't get along. But I'm already slipping behind the hefty mortgage payment, and I'm using charge cards to stay afloat. How can I provide my children with the same standard of living?

The bottom line is—you can't. Unfortunately, this is one of the consequences of divorce. The sooner you accept that you need to adjust your spending, the easier it will be in the long run. If you continue in denial and use charge cards to maintain your lifestyle, when the bottom drops out, the crash will be severe.

Do your children really need a big house—or a peaceful home? Would they do best with a mom who is anxiety-ridden because of debt or with a relaxed mother whose priorities are in order?

Take a good look at what you are communicating to your children. They don't need things. They need you.

My former son-in-law has a sexual addiction. Although he has no history of abusing children, I can't believe my daughter is letting her three children, ages four through twelve, visit him unsupervised. Her lawyer said she couldn't withhold visitation. Isn't there anything we can do to keep the children away from him?

In most states, you must provide proof of endangerment to a child to stop parental visitation. A pornography problem isn't reason enough to prevent the father from seeing his children.

Consult a second attorney and share your concerns. Then consult a counselor who specializes in working with children, sexual abuse, and sexual addictions to ask what issues, if any, should be discussed with the children before they visit their dad. At the very least, they'll need to know how to respond if they see any pornography while visiting him.

My daughter left her husband to pursue a lesbian lifestyle. She moved in with her girlfriend and wants the children to visit her. I don't hate my daughter, but my son-in-law and I want to

prevent these children from being exposed to this relationship. Is that legally possible?

Unless your grandchildren are in physical danger, no law will keep them from visiting their mother.

You and your son-in-law need to explain the situation to the children in an age-appropriate, loving, and patient way. Focus on the fact that we each make choices, and although you love your daughter, you don't agree with her choice. Share what you love about her and speak kindly of her to them. Don't insult, berate, or condemn your daughter or her girlfriend.

Discuss the issue of homosexuality and answer their questions honestly. Books and Web sites by those who have lived in the homosexual culture and now are free of that lifestyle will help you understand your daughter and how to pray for her. The book *101 Frequently Asked Questions About Homosexuality* by Mike Haley[5] is a great place to start. It will also help you to avoid rudeness, stereotypes, and cliché answers.

My ex-husband's girlfriend tells my children there's no God and the stories about Jesus aren't true. Their father knows what she's doing but chooses to ignore it. I'm infuriated that this stranger is allowed to influence my children. Legally, how can I keep her away from my kids?

You'd need to prove that your children are in danger and have evidence that exposing your child to atheistic or anti-Christian beliefs is harming them. Most courts won't even consider such a case.

Try a different approach. Throughout your children's lifetime, they'll encounter people of many faiths. Use this opportunity to teach them how to listen, discern, and compare other faiths to Christianity. Instruct them on what God says about false gods and the people who reject Jesus.

We live in a world that opposes Christ. Your children need to learn what they believe and why. Consistently explain your views, how you came to believe in God, and how your faith was strengthened with answered prayers.

Focus on the truth not the girlfriend. Be careful not to condemn her. Address why you don't agree with her view of atheism, rather than her personally.

This is a superb opportunity to display and share how to love someone who rejects Jesus. Ask God for a tender heart toward this woman, and seek the ability to see her as He sees her. Include her and your former spouse in family prayer time. If done sincerely, these actions will demonstrate that it's not our job, nor should we try, to force anyone to believe in Christ. Prayer will communicate to your children that we should have a deep burden for those who don't know Jesus as Savior.

Don't view her as a threat. As their mother, you have the privilege and responsibility to pray for and teach your children. The old saying that more is "caught" than "taught" is accurate. If you're teaching your children to love as Christ does, but your actions toward this woman are mean-spirited, guess which message they'll hear?

Holy Father,

The weight of financial burdens and legal decisions is crushing me. I don't know how I'm going to survive—there doesn't seem to

be any way out. I'm terrified of what the future holds and embar-
rassed to tell anyone the depth of my financial problems.

God, I need an attorney to help me with this mess. I don't know
where to turn for help or how to find one who will give me the
advice I need and yet not antagonize my spouse. Please guide and
direct me to the right person.

Your Word says Your ways are higher than mine and that You
think much more clearly than I do. I need Your thoughts, Your
way. I'm going to trust You because your Word says You know the
anguish of my soul. God, in each critical decision I must make,
show me what to do. Amen.

(Portions of this prayer are taken from Isaiah 55:8–9 and Psalm 31:7.)

Chapter 6 Questions

1. What are the sobering financial consequences of separation? Of divorce? What has been your biggest financial challenge since your separation or divorce?

2. What are some creative ways in which you can earn more money? Live on less money?

3. Which tips about finding and using an attorney did you find helpful? Explain your answer.

4. What's the balance between viewing God as your provider and hiring an attorney to represent your interests in a divorce?

5. The author wrote about "letting go of things over which you have no control." What are some examples of this?

6. What are the first steps a single person should take if he or she has been out of the workforce for a while and must work outside the home?

7. What are the benefits of going to a budget counselor? What excuses do people give for not seeking financial help?

8. Why do our motives matter so much as we make financial decisions?

To Do This Week ...

- Write down a realistic list of debts and income.
- Make an appointment with someone trustworthy who has good financial skills and who can help you discern the next steps toward financial stability.

7

How Did I Get Here?

CODEPENDENCY AND SELF-ESTEEM

Toto, I've a feeling we're not in Kansas anymore.
DOROTHY, *THE WIZARD OF OZ*

While opening a new can of bathroom cleanser, I automatically pulled the tab off the top and then re-stuck it over half of the holes. My mother and grandmother did the same thing. Why do I do that? My grandmother probably started the custom because she lived through the Depression and learned to be frugal. But let's face it: A can of cleanser isn't pricey these days, so that wasn't my motive. There's no logical reason for continuing the tradition I learned from them.

The patterns we've developed over our lifetimes are part of who we are. We make decisions and view life and ourselves based on what we learned and experienced during our formative years.

How we developed into the people we are today is a complex and intricate topic, one that I don't claim to be specialist in. However, after several years of divorce-recovery ministry, I observed a pattern. Many people who attended the group were struggling with codependency issues.

Pat Springle gives an excellent definition of codependency in his book *T\Rapha's Twelve-Step Program for Overcoming Codependency*. He says codependency is:

> A compulsion to control and rescue people by fixing their problems. It occurs when a person's God-given needs for love and security have been blocked in a relationship with a dysfunctional person, resulting in a lack of objectivity, a warped sense of responsibility, being controlled and controlling others.[1]

Codependency doesn't seem damaging because it's so familiar to us and it feels loving. But the truth is, it obstructs our thinking and clouds the danger ahead.

I have a confession to make: I'm codependent. In other words, I'm a rescuer—a fixer with a warped sense of responsibility. Early in my ministry, God showed me that I'd burn out quickly if I continued in this destructive behavior pattern. He revealed that it wasn't my job to rescue the people attending the support groups. Instead of assuming the burden of their trauma, I was to give them over to God. Getting out of the way and letting go is torture for a rescuer because it means loss of control, which can be frightening.

A person can become codependent or have low self-worth for many reasons. Often the two problems go hand-in-hand. Almost all codependent behavior in adults can be traced to the following problems that occurred in their childhood homes:

- Alcoholism or drug abuse anywhere within the family (including grandparents, stepparents, siblings, cousins, and so forth)

- Physical abuse (including being beaten, spat on, bitten, slapped, locked in the closet, and so forth)
- Emotional abuse (including being insulted, intensely criticized, told you were never wanted or you are stupid, and so forth)
- Sexual abuse by a relative, neighbor, or a close friend of the family
- Parents with extensive mental disorders
- Parents who were physically ill and unavailable
- Parents who were emotionally unavailable
- Parents who were absent due to a divorce or workaholism
- Parents who were unpredictable and yelled, screamed, and accused with no explanation
- Parents who used the child as a substitute for a mate
- Parents who coddled or overprotected the child
- Parents who expected perfection and unrealistic standards

It makes sense that if our needs aren't met as children, we gravitate toward someone or something to fill them. "The more deeply one has been wounded, the higher the probability that one will be codependent. The pain from the past leaks into the present," wrote John P. Splinter.[2]

For example, a girl who knew her father was unfaithful to her mother may have trust issues. A man who, as a boy, saw his mother beaten by her husband may gravitate toward needy women seeking rescue. A child raised in an alcoholic home in which everyone walked on eggshells around the alcoholic may have a "peace at all costs" mentality. And the little darling whose parents indulged her every whim will probably struggle with self-centeredness as an adult.

Wishing we could change the harmful effects of our past won't make them go away. Sometimes it's hard to make the connection, but those influences do have a profound effect on whom we become and whom we're prone to date. Divorce can be a crude wake-up call that forces us to investigate our past and the effect it has had on our decision-making skills.

Are you codependent? Ask yourself the following questions—and remember, most codependents don't think they have a problem. The behavior is habitual and feels normal, even loving. Do I:

- believe leniency is an expression of love?
- feel guilty if I say no?
- have a sense of dread, fear, or anger if I'm not in control of a situation?
- fear what others are thinking of me?
- make excuses for other people's poor choices and bad behavior?
- desire to solve others' problems?
- allow people to speak to me in a disrespectful manner?
- try to control others?

Answering yes to more than a couple of these questions could indicate that you might be codependent. Can you learn healthy behavior? Yes! It takes a willingness to roll up your sleeves and tackle the issue.

Saint Augustine said a God-shaped void is inside each of us. We try to deny that void or fill it with relationships, work, substances, money, and other things. But God is the only One who can fill the void. He alone can reveal the areas of codependency that may have affected your marriage. As you discover your own areas of weakness, you'll need to surrender issues one by one and ask for healing.

What happens if you decide to deny your codependency? Your future is at stake. Most people experiencing divorce say, "I don't ever want to go through this again." If this sounds like you, then I have one question: What will you do to discover and heal your brokenness?

One of the reasons my first marriage dissolved was because my own heart and self-worth were damaged by my parents' divorce. I wasn't able to give because my tank was empty. On the outside, I looked like a happy, outgoing, secure person. But on the inside, I was dying. I was needy. It wasn't until I admitted my weakness and got help that I began to heal.

What was it like being married to you? Think back and be honest. Were you miserable and moody? Did you explode when things didn't go your way? Were you clingy? Did you wallow in self-pity? Did your temperament resemble a roller coaster? Were you emotionally unavailable? Did you cower in a corner seeking scraps of praise? Did you make excuses for yourself and everyone else?

Why did you select your ex-spouse as a mate? What attracted you to him or her? What about you drew that person into a relationship? In what ways did you think that person would complete you or make you whole? Why did you choose to ignore certain behaviors? Did you think you could fix your ex-spouse?

These questions aren't intended to make you feel bad about yourself. The goal is just the opposite. You don't want to repeat the same destructive patterns. The honesty with which you answer and your willingness to identify trouble spots will determine the success of a second marriage.

The cure for our brokenness isn't finding the right person but *becoming* the right person. For most of us, this requires asking God to reveal the areas where we are broken, letting go of things we can't control, and desiring to become whole. The key to victory is for us to evaluate our willingness to heal. Familiar patterns are comfortable and they feel safe. Changing habitual behaviors can be frightening. The questions then become, *Am I tired of living this way? Am I willing to discover why I make the choices I do?*

Resources listed in the back of this book will help you explore the issue of codependency, setting healthy boundaries, and learning about safe people.

My first husband was controlling and cruel. I met my second husband at church, and he was charming, attractive, and kind. I thought he was a great catch. After six months of marriage, I've discovered he has a sexual addiction. How did I end up in another bad marriage?

You need to find out why you gravitate toward men with destructive behaviors. "Repeating the same behavior over and over but expecting different results" is one definition of codependency. A good counselor can explain why you're drawn to emotionally unhealthy people. You'll know you're overcoming the problem when you can recognize addicts and aren't attracted anymore.

Ask yourself, "What drew me to this person? Did I take the time to evaluate his true character? Did I ask sensible friends to evaluate his integrity? Why not? What indicators of his addiction did I choose to overlook? Why did I ignore the uncomfortable feelings I had about his choice of movies, TV shows, magazines, and books? Why would I ignore the fact that he gawks at other women? Do I believe a 'peace at all costs' mentality is virtuous?" The answers to these and other questions will help you gauge your level of codependency and begin to work to break it.

My husband doesn't think his drinking is a problem, but our electricity has been turned off twice because he used the money for booze. He drinks because he lost his last job and his new boss treats him badly. I've gotten a second job to help pay the bills, but now that I'm not home in the evening, he drinks even more. Even though I love my husband, I have decided to separate from him because I don't know how to fix his problem.

In your love and loyalty to your spouse, you're attempting to protect him from the consequences of his drinking. It won't work. You are enabling him by preventing him from experiencing the necessary crisis that could save him.

Your husband doesn't have a problem—he gets to do whatever he pleases. You, on the other hand, have a big problem. If you truly love him, the kindest thing you can do is to help him have a problem. That may sound odd, but it's true.

Al-Anon and similar support groups can help you understand alcoholism. They'll advise you on how to avoid the temptation to control the situation and will encourage you to let him suffer the consequences of his poor choices. This is tough love. God allows His beloved children to suffer consequences of their choices. The Bible is filled with illustrations: Adam and Eve, King David, Jonah, and the rich young ruler are just a few. Ask Him for the strength to help you show tough love to your husband.

My wife's spending habits are out of control. We make a good living, but because she refuses to limit her spending, we're deeply in debt. I've reprimanded, lectured, and threatened, but nothing seems to work. I'm thinking of leaving her if she doesn't stop.

A habitual spending pattern might indicate that your wife gets a "high" from her purchases. Ask God to reveal to you why she's addicted to spending. Encourage her to see a counselor who can help her.

If she chooses not to go, then you need to take more drastic action. In *Boundaries in Marriage,*[3] Henry Cloud and John Townsend suggest spouses remove credit cards, open separate accounts, and stop payments so they are no longer held accountable for the money their partners spend.

Threatening divorce will further break down the communication and trust in your marriage. It won't solve this problem. Don't give up on your marriage.

My sister has brought tremendous grief to our family by leaving her husband and children. At gatherings, she brings the new boyfriend, acts like nothing is wrong, and gets angry if we mention the situation. My mother wants us to sweep it under the rug and be happy together, but I just can't do it. How can I get my sister to acknowledge her actions and apologize for the pain she has caused us?

You can't force another person to recognize or repent of her actions. Trying to control your sister's response is only frustrating you not her. Until she decides to address the situation, you can't do anything. It appears she hasn't suffered the consequences of her actions yet, and therefore she expresses no remorse.

Lowering your expectations can diminish the anger you feel. Focus on the things or people you can influence, such as the children. Your nieces and nephews need you now more than ever. Their mother has abandoned them, and this rejection will leave a deep scar. Look for practical ways you can be a part of their lives and help their dad.

My brother won the custody of his two little girls when his wife left him. My initial response was to distance myself because I couldn't bear to see their broken little hearts hurt so much. But instead, God gave me the strength to help them. During the week, I'd go to his home and help the girls get ready for school and day care. I listened to their struggles and fears and helped them face the day. I read Bible verses to them each morning and prayed that God's Word would penetrate their lives. My goal was to fill some of the gaps in their lives as they coped with the loss of their mother. I knew anger wouldn't help my nieces, so I asked God to help me see my ex-sister-in-law as He sees her. God transformed my mind so I was able to have compassion for her. I encourage you to pray for your sister and allow God to help you see her through His eyes.

My wife has had two extramarital affairs. Both times she returned to our marriage, I gave her new clothes and jewelry to demonstrate my forgiveness. Now she is lying again and involved in another relationship. How can I get her to stop?

What consequences has your wife suffered for breaking the marriage covenant? Are you aware that you've rewarded her for committing adultery? Without a moral breakthrough or damaging consequence, she has no reason to stop having affairs. She believes she has the best of both worlds.

Ask yourself why you're rewarding her for her behavior. My guess is that if we drill down to the bottom of this destructive situation, you may find that fear is motivating you. You may be afraid of confronting your wife because this unhealthy relationship fills a vacuum inside of you. This behavior will continue until you learn how to break the cycle. Allowing infidelity to continue without severe consequences doesn't demonstrate love. You can't "get her to stop" as you asked, but you can create an outcome that validates your desire for a healthy marriage. Just as God loves us too much to look the other way when we sin, you should not pretend that the marriage covenant is intact.

My husband slaps and punches me when he gets mad. He says he's sorry afterward and promises it won't happen again, but it does. He says it's my fault, and if I were a better Christian wife I'd know how to submit. I don't know what to do.

You can't see them, but the hairs on the back of my neck are standing up. Other than child abuse, few things disturb me more than Scripture being twisted to defend sin. Unfortunately, people often use God's Word to justify domestic violence. I'm certain it makes Him weep.

So let's clarify the truth. God hates for women to be beaten, abused, or murdered just as much as He hates divorce. You are God's precious child. Your husband has an enormous problem with anger, and he needs help immediately. This has nothing to do with submission and everything to do with his problem. His actions aren't your fault; you won't stop him from beating you by allowing it to continue.

You must get help. Start with your church leaders. If they ignore the request or don't believe you, ask a friend from another church if she knows a church that will help. Don't let anyone convince you it's wrong to seek protection. If your husband has isolated you from family and friends, call a domestic-violence hotline for information on how to escape your home safely. Prepare beforehand for your husband's rage! You will reveal his sin, and he won't be happy about it. You'll need to stay away from the home until he admits he has a serious problem and after he gets help with anger management.

If you have children, you'll need to get them into counseling too. They've been traumatized by seeing their father hurt their mother. Experienced, professional counselors will know how to help you and your children break the cycle of abuse before it continues to the next generation.

Now that I'm divorced, church members assume I'm able to work on every committee and task. I try to say no, but then I feel guilty when no one else is available. Why can't I say no and stick to it?

You can't say no because you're afraid they'll be mad at you and/or think less of you. It's easy to spot people who can't say no: Guilt or intimidation dictates their behavior. If you'd like to learn how to break this pattern, attend a *Boundaries* class (see resources). Start by setting boundaries with a safe, emotionally healthy person. Pick someone who will hear your no and won't respond with rejection. The resistant or controlling person will be more difficult to deal with and will require more strength.

Before setting a boundary with an unsafe person, plan how you'll react to his resentment. The first few times you attempt this, it won't be easy.

A man came to me one day with this problem. He had custody of his son, and his ex-wife was coming into town for the son's graduation. She assumed it would be all right to stay at his home. He wasn't comfortable with this arrangement, but the thought of confronting her made him ill.

I helped him create a reasonable boundary. I suggested he offer to give her a list of phone numbers of local hotels. When she said she assumed she was staying with him, he told her he didn't think that would be wise, and repeated his offer to give her the list of phone numbers. It took courage, but he did it. She was so shocked by his firm, controlled response that she agreed to his offer.

If she had fought harder, he was prepared. We discussed how to say no in a clear and unyielding manner without letting the conversation turn into a fighting match.

Remember Bill Murray in the movie *What About Bob?* His entire journey was to take baby steps toward overcoming his fears. This guy had every paranoia known to man. I love the scene where he yells, "I'm sailing, I'm sailing!" As the camera pulls back, the audience sees that he is roped, strapped, and almost glued to the mast of the boat— but he is indeed sailing.

In the beginning, this is what setting boundaries will feel like. It's threatening and foreign. But when you realize that it's okay—and sometimes wise—to say no, you'll conquer your fear.

Heavenly Father,

I need You to heal the wounds that cause me to make poor decisions. Reveal to me areas where I've been conditioned to think in unhealthy ways. Lord, help me surrender to You any addiction, whether to people, behavior, or substances. I want freedom but don't know how to find it.

Help me to recognize the difference between being loving and being codependent. I know You want me to have a healthy mind filled with peace. Your Word tells me the way to have this contentment is to stay focused on You and Your truth, because You can be trusted.

Lord, You alone know my innermost thoughts. You know how they got there and why. You created me. Before a word comes out of my mouth, You know it.

Help me, dear God. Heal me. Touch my life and fill it with Your goodness.

(Portions of this prayer are taken from Isaiah 26:3 and Psalm 139:1–2, 4.)

Chapter 7 Questions

1. What is codependency, and what effects does it have on the codependent person? On people in relationship with the codependent person?

2. During childhood, what are some things that can cause a person to become codependent and/or have a low self-worth? What childhood events shaped how you view yourself?

3. What's the difference between being loving and being codependent? Between being too lenient and showing mercy?

4. How can a person start replacing codependent behaviors with healthy behaviors?

5. What was it really like to be married to you? Or, if you are separated, to still be married to you? Why is it important for each
   of us to identify trouble spots and stop repeating destructive patterns? What will you avoid in the future?

6. Why is it scary to try to change our destructive, habitual behaviors? How will you move forward in changing any destructive
   patterns you have?

7. Which question-and-answer section(s) in this chapter caused
   you to react? Why?

8. What does it mean to demonstrate "tough love" toward an
   addicted spouse? Why do people who do wrong things need to
   suffer the consequences of their actions?

To Do This Week ...

- Ask a trusted same-sex friend what things he or she recognizes in you that may be causing problems in present
  relationships.
- Consider professional counseling if you have unresolved
  wounds from the past.

8

Nobody Understands

FAMILY AND FRIENDS

They dress the wound of my people as though it were not serious.

GOD

I've been involved with divorce recovery for a long time, but I'm still flabbergasted by the things people say and do to those who are divorcing. Imagine you've just had open-heart surgery. A friend comes to visit and, upon approaching your bedside, gives you a hearty punch in the chest. Is this likely to happen? No, probably not. But that's exactly what many people do to someone who's had a divorce. The hurtful words and actions other people often inflict cause more heartache than the divorce itself.

As kids we shouted, "Sticks and stones can break my bones, but words will never hurt me." It's a lie. Words do injure us and penetrate the most vulnerable part of who we are. Unfortunately, our brains don't purge these toxic thoughts. Instead, we tend to relive the blows to an already fragile sense of self-worth.

Why do people say and do hurtful things? It could be from ignorance, a need to fill the awkward silence, guilt, and fear of suffering the same pain. Or it could be insensitivity, tongues that move faster than brains, foolishness, a desire to preach, an inclination to hurt others, stupidity, or revenge.

The bottom line is that not everyone is going to be helpful, kind, or gentle with your wound, including Christians. The way to protect yourself is to lower your expectations and prepare for those who might not respond the way you wish they would.

We've all said things we wish we could take back, especially in situations we're unfamiliar with. But even if years have passed, it's never too late to return to someone and apologize for insensitive comments.

My husband has been living a double life with another woman for over a year. I found bank accounts and other legal documents in both their names. My mother keeps saying that if I had been a better wife, housekeeper, and cook, he wouldn't have left. Her words are haunting me. What could I have done to keep him?

Your husband has gone to great lengths to create a double life. The intense spiritual and emotional issues that cause a person to behave this way couldn't have been corrected with a cleaner toilet or better spaghetti sauce. He needs professional help.

I'm sorry one of the most significant people in your life is pouring salt into your wound. Your mother should be a source of comfort. She doesn't appear to understand your pain.

Your first priority is to guard your heart. You're grieving a severe loss, and her comments are unacceptable. If your mother continues to speak to you in this hurtful manner, set a firm boundary with her. Tell her you'll have to limit the time you spend with her if she doesn't stop criticizing your role as a wife. If she persists, you have no choice but to stop visiting her. Don't feel guilty—she's accountable for her choices.

Surround yourself with godly praying women who understand your pain and can help you through this difficult time.

After my husband left our three children and me, I had no choice but to move back home with my parents. When my ex-husband comes to pick up the kids for visitation, my mother gives him dirty looks and makes snide comments. Since my parents are supporting us financially, I feel I can't say anything to her.

It's wise that you recognize your mother's behavior as inappropriate. Many parents encourage the grandparents to treat the ex-spouse with disdain. But this has a long-term, harmful effect on children.

When your kids are away, share your concerns with your mom. Start by acknowledging that you are sorry for her heartache and you recognize that the divorce has affected her life, too. Explain your goal to become a godly single parent so your children can grow up in a stable home. Tell her you need her help. Clarify that successful single parents don't condemn or insult the other parent because it damages their children's self-worth. Help her understand that when she criticizes their father, she's harming them, because their father is a part of them. For example, if your mother says he's lazy, the children interpret this to mean, "Since I'm a part of my father, I must be lazy too."

If she continues to insult him, then you might have to arrange for them to meet their dad at another location. Also, remove them from the room every time she starts this type of talk. She must understand that you're serious. Don't underestimate the impact of this destructive conduct; you'll need to make other living arrangements as soon as possible to protect your children.

> **My wife wants a divorce, and I'm praying she'll change her mind. My younger sister, who has never married, keeps nagging me to fight for everything we own. Sharing the names of lawyers who have reputations for being "barracudas" is her latest attempt. I don't want to antagonize my wife. Why can't my sister leave the situation alone?**

If your sister has no history of controlling behavior, then my guess is she's responding to your pain. In the same way you'd react if you saw someone punching your sister, she sees her big brother being emotionally beaten up, and her instincts are telling her to fight back. Her only resource is her mouth.

Tell her you understand her concern and appreciate the support. Explain that you're praying about the situation and trusting God to guide your decisions—including the legal ones. Thank her for wanting to help, but tell her you need her to stop interfering. If she continues, remind her as needed.

As an alternative, let her know how she can help you during this difficult time. Many times, people need suggestions on how they can demonstrate their love. If after all this, she still won't stop, you'll have no choice but to limit the time you spend with her.

> **While in my lawyer's office for the first time, I asked him if he'd ever been divorced. With a look of disgust and a tone of revulsion, he replied, "Of course not." I felt as though he viewed me as a piece of scum. Why would a divorce lawyer act this way?**

I don't have a clue. Maybe he doesn't need clients. At the very least, he's not very bright. His ability to look down his nose at those who are divorcing tells me he won't represent you well. I'd get a new lawyer. Pronto!

When I told one of my closest friends about my husband leaving, she said, "It takes two to get divorced. You must have done something to drive him away." Her comments hurt almost as much as the divorce. Why would she say such a cruel thing?

Several reasons come to mind. The first and most probable is that she believes the adage "it takes two." You and I know that isn't always true. It takes two to get married but only one to get divorced.

Another possibility is that she's never experienced this pain and doesn't understand how devastating it is. In his book *Successful Single Parenting,* Gary Richmond states, "No form of rejection begins to compare with divorce."[1]

A third option may be that she's fearful about her own marriage. If it's on shaky ground, this may have been a quick, flippant response to help her cope with the thought that one day she might be in the same situation.

Don't dwell on why she said it. Avoid her during this time of crisis. And then when you aren't as emotionally wounded, share with her how those comments hurt you. Talk it out, and then let it go.

Since my divorce, the husband of one of my closest friends has been "coming on to me." I don't want to lose my friend, so I haven't said anything to her. I don't know what to do.

I've heard that cockroaches come out of the walls as soon as it gets dark. You're dealing with one of them. This man thinks it's safe to prey on a vulnerable woman because she no longer has her husband's protection.

Tell this predator you won't tolerate his actions. Explain that you refuse to ignore his inappropriate behavior.

Then you must decide whether to tell his wife. I believe telling her is the right thing to do. Ask yourself, "If I were in her shoes, would I want to know?" If you're like me, the answer is yes, but not every woman wants to know the truth about her husband.

If you decide to inform your friend, be specific about times, places, and details. Prepare for the possibility that she might not believe you or that she might blame you. She may accuse you of enticing her husband. This initial response is common, but her choice to ignore the truth doesn't change the fact that it needs to be told.

You may temporarily lose her as a friend, but over time she may understand that you needed to be honest. If her husband's conduct doesn't change, you can be certain there will be other complaints.

My spouse decided to end our fourteen-year marriage. I tried to stop the divorce, but now the marriage is over. A church leader told me that because I'm divorced, God could no longer use me. Is this true?

If our works determine our usefulness to God, none of us could pass muster. We've all failed Him. To say divorce eliminates our value to God infers that divorce is more powerful than Christ and the price He paid for you. Is anything more powerful than the blood of Christ? No.

God hates divorce because it damages His beloved people, but He doesn't hate you. God still sees you as His delightful, gifted, extraordinary creation. He doesn't see "reject" stamped on your forehead.

In John 4:4–42, Jesus revealed to the Samaritan woman that He knew she'd had five husbands—not counting the man she was living with. Then He told her that He was the long-awaited Messiah. She ran back to town and told everyone, and they went to see for themselves. Verse 39 says, "Many of the Samaritans from that town believed in him because of the woman's testimony."

So I ask you, did Jesus use this sinful woman who had five husbands? Why didn't He go into town and use one of the more reputable people? God sees our heart. He didn't see *what* she was; He saw *who* she was—His treasured bride.

Humble yourself before God and ask Him if there's anything in the marriage or divorce for which you need to seek forgiveness. Then let it go. Offer all of the brokenness, hurt, and anguish to Him. God will give a purpose to your pain. It's His specialty! You'll be amazed at how He will take this dark season in your life and turn it into a blessing for others. I can say this for certain, because He did it for me.

My husband left our marriage for a homosexual relationship. I feel so stupid when people actually say to me, "You mean you didn't know?" The truth is, I didn't know because he was deceptive and an excellent liar. Don't they understand that this comment hurts?

They probably are genuinely puzzled and don't understand they're hurting you. You may be surprised that people also make this comment to a person who discovers his or her spouse is leading a double life of any kind. For acquaintances, a simple "No, I didn't know" will suffice. For those who know you well, adding "and the deception has been very painful" should help them get the picture.

Don't dwell on the comments. You aren't stupid. The rejection and dishonesty have attacked your self-worth and ability to think clearly. A support group and resources on homosexuality such as those listed in the back of this book will help you understand this complex issue and dilute the impact of ignorant statements.

> **After my husband left our marriage, my longtime Christian friend invited me to dinner. Before the meal arrived she said, "Because you are getting divorced, we can no longer be friends. Divorce is contagious, and I can't allow my husband and me to be around you any longer." I was so stunned I couldn't think or eat. I don't know how, but I held back the tears until I got to the car. Why would she respond this way?**

I suspect the reason is because deep in her heart, she knows her own marriage is in trouble. Running away from you keeps her fear at bay; she can stuff it down a little further. Your pain is a reminder that she might experience the same thing one day.

Another less likely reason might be that she prefers friendships that are superficial—neat and tidy and without complications or crises. Or she may have such a judgmental attitude that she avoids those she views as "untouchable" because they may damage her image.

Regardless of her reasons, pray for her. A woman who would drop a friend in crisis has serious issues of her own. Then start building friendships with women who want a deeper, more sincere relationship.

My wife left our marriage, and my buddies keep saying, "Get on with your life" or "Just get over her." It's not that easy. I love her and I want her back. Why do they think it's so simple?

We live in a society where Hollywood stars get married and remarried more quickly than most people eat a Happy Meal at McDonald's. The institution of marriage isn't valued as it once was. It's viewed as Velcro instead of Super Glue. Therefore many people don't realize that the covenant between husband and wife is a unique and precious gift, and when it's ripped apart, the pain is excruciating.

Another reason your friends may be reacting this way is that it's troubling them to see you hurting and they don't know how to help. Suggesting you find a new woman is their way of affirming you. Explain your grief and the difficulty of this pain and loss. Share some of the things you need right now, such as help moving or ideas about making extra money. True friends will follow through.

Dear God,

No one seems to understand my pain. The reactions I'm receiving from people, even those who are supposed to love and support me, are hurtful. Lord, I need Your wisdom in how to respond. Show me if there are relationships I need to sever or put on hold. Help me to recognize that my friends may avoid me because they don't understand this pain. I need to accept that not everyone is going to be kind or helpful. Guide me to new friends who can help me walk through this season of life.

Lord, You are acquainted with rejection; therefore, You know how to respond. Show me how to pray for those who have hurt me. Teach me how to forgive. I need You.

Thank You, Jesus, for never leaving me. Amen.

(Portions of this prayer are taken from Psalm 38:11; Isaiah 53:3; Matthew 20:18–19; and 26:49, 74.)

CHAPTER 8 QUESTIONS

1. What misconceptions did you have about separation/divorce before it happened to you?
2. What kinds of hurtful things have people said or done to you concerning your marital situation? If you feel comfortable doing so, share several of these.
3. What is involved in establishing a firm boundary with someone who is hurting you? Why should we hold people accountable for their choices—including choices that hurt us?
4. When one parent criticizes or insults the other parent, how does that affect their children?
5. As you read about people who say or do hurtful things, what did you realize about their motives? What are some ways in which you could effectively communicate to these people and help them gain more understanding of divorce's impact?
6. Why do you think the author encourages us to pray for people who hurt us? To forgive those people? Will you forgive those who have hurt you? Why, or why not?
7. How can we remember that God sees us "as his delightful, gifted, extraordinary creation" even when we don't feel very valuable?

What does the story about Jesus' interaction with the Samaritan woman (John 4:4–42) reveal about His heart?

8. Are you willing to allow God to turn your dark seasons of life into blessings for others? Why, or why not?

9. When former friends put us down and even sever our relationships with them, how can we find new friends who want deep, sincere relationships with us?

To Do This Week …

- Get two pieces of paper or two sticks and superglue them together. Show them to a family member or friend and ask them to tear the items apart. Pieces of one side will end up sticking to the other. Use this illustration as a way to share that this is what divorce feels like. It's not a clean break. It hurts.

9

Santa's Stuck in the Chimney

HOLIDAYS, SPECIAL OCCASIONS,
AND FORMER IN-LAWS

Holidays are an expensive trial of strength.
The only satisfaction comes from survival.
JONATHAN MILLER

Christmas. We envision a Norman Rockwell scene and can almost smell the cinnamon of freshly baked pies and the rich aroma of pipe tobacco. We visualize chattering ladies donning white aprons and Grandma as she proudly positions her poultry masterpiece in the center of the table. A longing fills our hearts as we desire to embrace the warmth, love, and community that surround this family banquet. And a little voice whispers, "If only this scene were true in my life."

For most people, a few bars of "Have Yourself a Merry Little Christmas" can evoke nostalgia, but for those in the turmoil of marital separation, it goes much deeper. Christmas and other holidays recall better, more pleasurable times.

When I was a child, Christmas Eve was an elaborate event in my dad's Italian family. For that special night, my nana prepared an exceptional menu of meats, fish, pastas, and pastries that would make angels salivate. My cousins, aunts and uncles, godparents, and various other people filled the house with boisterous talking, bellowing laughter, and an occasional argument. Nana's girlfriends spoke only Italian, and they smelled a little odd. But their pinch to your cheek or bone-crunching hug that could cause a body builder to wince only added to the fun.

The movie *My Big Fat Greek Wedding* brings back wonderful memories of the holidays at Nana's. It causes me to recall a time when I belonged to something bigger than myself. I felt loved and safe.

Now Nana is gone, the house is sold, and the family is scattered. My quest to find meatballs like hers has proven fruitless, and I'll never again walk into her fragrant kitchen that whispered, "Welcome home."

The holidays have a way of triggering all sorts of memories. And when divorce strikes, every light you string, stocking you hang, and card you read is a reminder that everything is different now.

The good news is you can create new traditions. Learning what to expect, how to prepare and respond, and what sights and sounds trigger painful emotions can help to keep depression from taking over.

Here are some ways to make Christmas special despite your circumstances:

- Discern when your spouse's absence will be most painful. For example, a vacant spot at the table, Christmas morning breakfast, or a family tradition. Plan new traditions or special activities for these times.
- Start new, meaningful traditions. Have a slumber party, make handmade decorations or gifts, visit a nursing home.
- Develop a coping strategy. Review whom to call or where to go if the stress or pain becomes too severe. Don't hibernate

or wait until the day before Christmas to make a plan. Force yourself to be with other people, even if it's only briefly.

- Review the visitation schedule with your ex spouse and children at least one week in advance. This will help you avoid any surprises and alleviate any fears your kids may be experiencing.

- Help your child buy a small gift for your ex-spouse and his or her parents. This communicates your permission to your child to love the other family, and it eases tension.

- If you're feeling suicidal, seek help immediately. The phone number of your counselor, pastor, close friend, or hotline should be taped to your phone. Don't minimize the effect the holidays can have on your mental state.

- Don't anesthetize your pain with drugs or alcohol. These chemicals induce depression, which leads to a greater sense of isolation.

- Say no! Let someone else orchestrate the Christmas pageant, plan the school play, or sing in the choir. Repeat after me: "I'm sorry, I'm not able to make cookies for the exchange this year."

- Take care of your physical well-being. Exercise and eat healthy, nourishing foods. Such things are natural stress reducers.

- Connect with a support group. They often have fun holiday activities.

- Budget for the holidays. Evaluate how much money is available for gifts and don't overspend. If this is an area of weakness for you, or if guilt or depression is motivating your purchases, use cash instead of credit cards.

- Reach out to people who are alone during the holidays, such as exchange students, other singles, the elderly, and those staying in homeless shelters.

- Do something completely different this year. Visit an out-of-state friend, take a cruise, go to the mountains or the beach, go skiing or hiking.
- Treat yourself to cozy bed linens in a magnificent color. A new pillow can work wonders for neck tension.
- Get sunshine. Winter's shorter daylight hours can take their toll on our emotions. If you work where there are few windows, take a walk during lunch or on your break.
- Try these stress-fighting tips. Take a walk on a still, winter night. Stroll through a greenhouse or flower shop. Get a massage. Buy a cozy nightgown. Try stretching or neck exercises. Get a manicure or pedicure. Make yourself a warm, comforting drink such as cocoa or herb tea. Watch a funny movie. Try your hand at drawing or sculpting. Construct a model airplane. Get out the hammer and build something. Assemble an old train set. Attend a basketball game or car show.
- Look at a nativity scene and ponder the life represented by each figure. Put yourself into the sandals of a person present that night. Can you hear Mary's cry as she goes through labor pains? Do you observe the sweat on Joseph's brow as he helps her? Does the brilliance of the star cause you to squint? Then lift the Holy Child out of the manger and recognize the Lover of your soul. He left heaven because you were worth it. His love is that intense, that passionate, and that perfect.

Christmas isn't the only season when a divorced person struggles with melancholy. Graduations, weddings, birthday parties, and family reunions can prompt dispirited thoughts. These events and others have a profound ability to remind us that nothing will be as it once was.

I invited my ex-husband to join us for Christmas dinner because I felt I was over the pain, and I wanted my grown children and their families to have a nice holiday. He acted as though nothing had changed and we were still one big happy family. Now everyone's gone and I'm in worse shape than before. I tried to do the right thing—what happened?

Having the whole family around the dining-room table produced a warm sense of happier times. Then the stark reality of your new singleness hit like ice water when they left, and the emptiness and loneliness resurfaced. This is normal.

Preparing beforehand is the way to survive these emotions. They won't disappear, but you won't be ambushed by grief.

Next time, evaluate why you feel obligated to invite your ex-spouse to dinner. Ask yourself if you're doing it because of guilt, because family members are pressuring you, because you think God will view you as unloving if you don't, or if because saying no implies you haven't forgiven him. The answers to these questions will help you discern if it's wise to invite him again.

Christmas is fast approaching, and every time I attempt a trip to the mall, I fall apart emotionally. I cry as soon as I hear the familiar music and see the holiday trimmings. I feel like a fool and don't know what to do.

Christmas stirs emotions to a peak anyway, but when you add a severe loss to the mix, it's almost intolerable. If the mall or stores generate pain, then I suggest shopping by mail or the Internet this year. And give gift certificates instead of wrapped presents. Don't worry about not giving the perfect gift. Your mental health is more important than a present, and most people will understand that this holiday is difficult for you.

My kids keep asking, "When are we going to get a Christmas tree and start decorating the house like we have every other year?" Each ornament brings back memories of happier times, and I just can't get in the mood.

Kids love the holidays. They're also hoping that those traditions and tinsel will revive what they've lost.

Explain the situation to a few close friends or people from your divorce-recovery group. Ask them to conspire with the kids to "surprise" you with a decorated home, or invite them over to help with decorations. Then your kids will have someone to keep them occupied when you need a break. If your children notice you've been crying, explain that you're a bit sad, but it will pass. Then help your children focus on something Christmassy that will distract them.

Start new traditions. Ask other families what fun customs they most enjoy. Review ideas in magazines, books, and other cultures. Who says Christmas dinner has to have mashed potatoes and gravy?

I'm dreading Christmas. My ex-wife is demanding that she have the children for most of the holiday. My parents have always had a big family dinner on Christmas Eve, and I feel guilty and angry that the kids might miss it.

Holidays and special occasions are difficult because they present another opportunity for control issues to arise. If one person is determined to "win" the kids for the holidays, it's more stressful. Obviously, your wife knows your family has this tradition. Try to speak calmly with her about the situation. The sooner you speak with her, the better—don't wait until a few days before the holidays to address the issue.

When you've decided on a schedule, explain it to your children. Again, to alleviate their fears, it's best that they know this well in advance. Your conversation should be enthusiastic and optimistic.

If you're unable to see your children on the holiday, plan for a special day soon after. Often children are so exhausted by Christmas that they enjoy a second event even more than they would the actual day. Try to incorporate your parents into your plans so they and your children get some special time together. Perhaps next year it will be easier and you can alternate the locations.

On most birthdays, our family tradition is to pull out old photo albums and reminisce. The pictures that once brought me joy now make me furious and miserable. I'm considering cutting my ex-spouse out of them, including my wedding pictures. Is this wrong?

Resist the temptation to grab the scissors and start cutting. As the years pass, you'll want to have pleasant memories of earlier times. And if you have children, they need to see that Mom and Dad were happy at one time. My parents divorced when I was eight, but I love to look at their wedding photo. I have no memory of them smiling together, but those pictures reveal that at one time things were better, and I was conceived in love.

If the temptation to destroy photos is strong, give them to a trusted friend for safekeeping until the urge to destroy them subsides.

Every year, my ex-husband and I hosted a big New Year's Eve bash. Now that I'm divorced, I feel estranged from the people who typically attended our annual party. The apprehension about that night is already starting to brew. Any suggestions?

Don't stay home alone, but plan ahead of time to be with family or friends. If that isn't an option, check the schedule of local churches or community groups.

This is an example of why it's essential to become part of a divorce-recovery group. Many of them hold events such as New Year's Eve parties to help with the emotions that can accompany the holidays. If you don't plan ahead, you may find yourself too drained to make last-minute arrangements. Going to a movie (nothing romantic or sad), ice skating, or out to dinner with a friend will help to keep those memories at bay.

My only grandson is about to have his first birthday, and my son and daughter-in-law are planning a big party. My ex-husband and the "other woman," whom he married shortly after our divorce, will be attending. I shared with my son that I'm uncomfortable with this situation, but he says I need to "get over it." What should I do?

One of the many stressful post-divorce issues is how to handle family gatherings. Your apprehension about this is not out of the ordinary. Your son's response shows that he's either unaware or in denial of how complicated this encounter is for you. You have a few options. You could visit your grandson before or after the others arrive or spend time alone with him on another day. I don't see these as the best choices because as other events arise you'll need to confront these emotions. However, if your pain is too fresh, it may be the wisest choice for now.

If you decide to attend the party, ask friends ahead of time to pray for you during the event and share with them the specific situations you're dreading. Have a friend available after the party to discuss how it went. When unexpected emotions send you reeling, that's when you're most vulnerable. You can minimize emotional turmoil by thinking through the situation before it arrives.

A cordial hello to your ex-husband and his wife is sufficient—and necessary to put other guests at ease. Seeing them together might stab your heart. Take a deep breath and ask God for strength. Focus on something else, or busy yourself in the kitchen with other guests. Don't dwell on the couple.

Remember, your son and his family are also victims of this circumstance. They're in the awkward position of entertaining family who are angry with each other. The smoother the event goes, the better it is for them.

Ultimately, the only way for this situation to improve is through forgiveness. God's grace can show you how to forgive them and yourself. Although the situation will never be perfect, forgiveness is the key for you to enjoy family gatherings regardless of who attends.

My ex-father-in-law has passed away, and I don't know if I should attend the funeral. What's the right thing to do?

Funerals are for the living. Therefore, it might not be appropriate to attend if your presence would cause further tension to the family, if your ex-spouse has remarried and you know it would cause stress, if your children would feel disloyal or torn between two parents, if the relationship between you and the ex-family isn't good, or if your relationship with the deceased wasn't good.

If you're unsure of your motive or if you can't resolve the issue, review the circumstances with a wise friend. An outsider can often evaluate the situation more clearly than family.

My daughter is getting married soon and has invited her father to the wedding. He left us when she was a small girl and hasn't been much support. I don't want to be in family pictures with him. What should I do?

If you love your child, you won't put added stress on her during this precious day. The most supportive thing you can do is to tell her, "I know there could be awkward situations at the wedding and reception. I want you to know that you don't have to worry. You just tell me what's best for you, what your desire is, and I'll be happy to comply." And then follow through on your words!

All children crave peace between their mom and dad. Although your ex-husband hasn't been a loyal dad, your daughter may still want him to be a part of her wedding. You need to give your daughter permission to extend love and courtesy to her father, even if you don't feel he deserves it. Do whatever it takes to go the extra mile and be considerate. She'll appreciate you for releasing her from the stress and guilt.

Smile and concentrate on your beloved daughter. You can do it.

My sister is getting married in a few months, and I just went through a difficult divorce. She wants me to be a bridesmaid, but I'm concerned about bursting into tears during the ceremony. What should I do?

Only you can answer this one. It's possible that by the time of the wedding you'll have your emotions under control, but it's hard to determine from this vantage point.

I dreaded going to the first wedding after my divorce. It was impossible to listen to my friend and her fiancé recite their vows without remembering the day my ex-husband promised to love, honor, and cherish me. The bride was a good friend who had bought my wedding dress from me. Seeing her in the dress only made the event more difficult, and I left shortly after dinner. I was happy for her, but I didn't have an enjoyable day.

Sit down with your sister and share your concerns. Tell her how honored you are to be her bridesmaid and that you want to be in the wedding but aren't sure you'll be ready emotionally. Together, you can find a solution. Remember that someone who hasn't experienced divorce may find it difficult to understand the pain involved. Ultimately, you must guard your heart. If you can't do it, say no. If she's angry with you, pray that in time she'll understand.

My former brother-in-law is getting married soon and has asked my young daughter to be in the wedding. She's thrilled, and I get along well with my former in-laws, but I'm feeling uncomfortable about attending such an intimate event with my ex-spouse and his new girlfriend present. What can I do to make it easier?

I have a friend who had to cope with this complicated situation. She handled it so beautifully that a person in the wedding party said to her afterward, "I heard you were a godly woman, but today I saw grace in action. Most women couldn't have done this, but you were wonderful." After keeping her emotions in check all day, his kind words caused her to burst out crying.

I asked her how she survived such an emotional day, and she replied, "I just focused on my daughter and how precious she looked. When the pastor recited the vows, I cried inside and thought, *Yeah ... my ex-husband said those words to me once.* But I refused to let my mind remain there."

If your separation or divorce happened recently, and you don't feel you'll be able to withstand the event, have a trusted family member take your daughter, and don't attend the wedding.

The date of my wedding anniversary is coming soon, and I'm not certain how I'm going to cope. What's the best way to handle that day?

There's no getting around it; your wedding anniversary can be difficult. In addition, friends and family members might not know whether to mention the date or contact you, not wanting to make it worse.

Who are the one or two special people in your life who allow you to be yourself? Contact those friends and share your apprehension. Then schedule a time on the anniversary date to get together and go out to dinner or a movie. Knowing that you have a plan will ease the anxiety.

Pray for the Lord to help you that day with negative thoughts. Replace them with God's promises for your future.

Dear God,

I'm dreading an upcoming event. I want to bury myself under the covers until it's over. But I'm also angry that this divorce has robbed me of holidays and special occasions. I can't even enjoy the normal things most people find enjoyable. Even blessed events have been spoiled by this horrible divorce. The things that used to make me happy now drive me deeper into depression. I need help.

Show me, Lord, how to start new traditions. Give me eyes to see these dates as celebrations of Your love. Please send friends to fill the lonely moments when my despair seems overwhelming. Help me to allow my kids to be happy even when I feel sad. Teach me how to rejoice with them when my own heart is heavy.

Please give me hope, Lord, that this won't last forever. Your Word says I may weep for a season, but rejoicing eventually comes. Lord, I need You to help me cling to this truth.

(Portions of this prayer are taken from Psalm 30:5.)

Chapter 9 Questions

1. What effect do memories of past holidays often have on divorced singles? Why? How have such memories affected you? How can you respond positively when things trigger sad memories for you?

2. Why is it essential for separated and divorced people to start new holiday traditions and do special activities during holidays?

3. Which people might you reach out to during the holidays?

4. If you could do something fun and different this year, what would you do? And what will it take to make such a dream happen?

5. Why do we need to keep evaluating our reasons for doing things, such as inviting an ex-husband over to Christmas dinner?

6. The author kept mentioning the importance of working out issues ahead of time, before the actual holidays. What keeps us from addressing potentially difficult issues? How can we overcome our inertia and make positive things happen? Why is it helpful to think through potentially difficult situations and plan ahead of time?

7. If you are not already in a divorce-recovery group, what's keeping you from participating in one? How might such a group help you during difficult times, such as memory-filled holidays and anniversaries?

8. Do you agree that forgiveness is the key to improving difficult situations with a separated spouse or ex-spouse? Why, or why not?

9. What did you think as you read about family-related weddings and the decisions that must be made? Did you agree with the advice given? Disagree? Why?

10. Why is it crucial for each of us to have several special friends who allow us to be ourselves and can provide wise counsel?

To Do This Week …

- If finances permit, consider Christmas shopping online by checking out any number of Web sites, including QVC.com.

- Look for others who may be hurting and reach out in a small way. Remember that divorce is not the only loss that causes pain. The death of a loved one, moving to a new location, or an illness can all cause loneliness and despair.

10

Is This Loneliness or Love?

DATING RELATIONSHIPS

God must rescue us from the very things we thought would save us.
JOHN ELDREDGE

If I had a gun right now, I'd shoot you and my ex-husband. No words were verbalized, but the hazardous thoughts charged through my brain. Sitting next to me was the unsuspecting gentleman who had asked me out on a date and then had the misfortune of my acceptance. My obnoxious mood resulted from my husband's recent abandonment. Why accept the invitation? The loneliness was overwhelming, and I naïvely assumed a date would be the cure. I was wrong.

Fortunately, I came to my senses and realized that asking my date to stop at a pawnshop to buy a gun might seem odd. The rest of the evening was uneventful, but I was eager for it to end.

My reentry into the dating scene didn't go very well, mostly because I attempted it too quickly. I can laugh at the memory now (I wonder whatever happened to that poor guy?), but I was definitely not laughing then. I detested the awkward adolescent feelings and resented having to return to the dating world. That stage of my life was supposed to be over. Dating forced me to admit the painful truth of my deceased marriage.

Adapting to the dating world again doesn't have to be painful. However, in the opinion of most experts in the divorce-recovery field, a minimum of two years after the divorce (not separation) is necessary for healing. However, this only applies to those who have attended a support group and worked hard to understand why the marriage ended. For those who choose not to get help, healing takes longer.

If timed properly and prepared for, dating again can be fun.

My divorce isn't final yet, but I've felt emotionally divorced for years. A wonderful Christian man who is everything I've ever hoped for has entered my life. Several friends say it's not right to date until I'm legally divorced. I disagree—it's only a piece of paper.

It's not uncommon to feel divorced even when there's no legal document. But this doesn't change the fact that in God's eyes you're still married. It's not a piece of paper, but a covenant. And married people don't date.

There are many reasons why waiting to date until you are legally single is wise. But one of the most compelling is the guilt you might experience years later if you don't wait. This was one of my own biggest regrets. I carried guilt for many years, wondering if my dating before the divorce was official communicated to my then-husband a lack of desire to reconcile.

I'm having a hard time discerning when I'll be ready to date again. Are there any guidelines?

An indication that you're ready to date is when you no longer dwell on the past marriage. More healing needs to take place if you continue to want to tell your divorce story, are avoiding or denying the true reasons why the marriage dissolved, or are blaming the former spouse for the marriage's demise.

The most accurate litmus test is when you can honestly say to yourself and to God, "I'm satisfied in my singleness. I don't require another person to make me happy or feel alive. God, You are all I need." This is the most significant evidence.

After I'd been separated for one month, a friend introduced me to a sweet man who was also divorcing. For two months, we've had a great time attending concerts, going to dinner, and dancing. Recently, he decided to go back to his wife. Now I'm grieving over my marriage and the loss of this great guy.

You're experiencing a hazard of dating someone not yet divorced. Dating numbed the heartache of divorce, but now the wound is worse because your loss has doubled. The grieving process starts all over again, and it will be more complicated.

Get an accountability partner to pray with you who understands your situation. When you're lonely and tempted to call your former boyfriend, call her instead. Recognize that the dating relationship will prolong your healing, and give yourself time to recover.

I met a beautiful woman who was separated from her husband. We had several months of bliss together, but now she and her husband have decided to restore their marriage. I know leaving

her alone is the right thing to do, but I can't stop thinking about her. I call and e-mail her constantly. Help!

Reconciling a marriage is difficult enough, but when a third person is introduced into the mix, it's even harder. If you care anything for this woman, you'll cease all contact with her immediately. Do whatever it takes to remove her from your thoughts. It won't be easy, but it's possible.

God understands the fierce struggle to forget her and He will help you. He wants your thoughts free of her more than you do. First Corinthians 10:13 (NLT) says, "The temptations in your life are no different from what others experience. And God is faithful. He will not allow temptation to be more than you can stand. When you are tempted, he will show you a way out so that you can endure." The question you must ask yourself is, *Am I searching and praying for a way to control my mind and actions?*

God will do His part. Will you do yours? The mind doesn't gravitate toward honorable thoughts willingly. "Take captive every thought to make it obedient to Christ" (2 Cor. 10:5). At first this might mean day-by-day, moment-by-moment replacing improper thoughts with holy ones. Eventually, this becomes easier to do. The battle is exhausting, but the results are gratifying.

I've been dating a nice guy for a few months. I'm not really attracted to him, but it's better than being alone. I'm starting to feel a little guilty. What should I do?

Shortly after my separation, I dated a younger guy who I didn't find attractive and with whom I had nothing in common. I couldn't bear the loneliness, so I used him to keep me company. How sad!

He also provided a way for me to prove to my friends and family that I was capable of getting another man. In my warped mind I was certain they were thinking, *She's such a loser no one will ever want her.* I now realize that was ridiculous, but at the time those thoughts felt very real.

Loneliness and pride are two deceitful reasons to date. It's wrong to use another human being this way.

Fill your loneliness and battered self-esteem with beneficial things rather than hurtful. You can explore new activities with same-sex friends. You'll be amazed at the abundant blessing these women can become in your life.

> **After being divorced for eight months, I've met the most beautiful and kind woman at church. Neither of us was looking for a new relationship, but we've fallen in love. We talk to each other for hours, something neither of us experienced in our former marriages. After dating for two months, we're discussing marriage. We both have young children from our previous marriages. Is there a length of time we should wait before getting engaged?**

Most people don't realize that when two people fall in love, their bodies produce chemicals that cause a euphoric state. This is often why we don't evaluate or see the new relationship as clearly as we should.

Although my response won't be popular, there are two key reasons why you should slow or even halt this relationship.

First, you haven't had time to fully grieve the loss of your previous marriage. I know you may feel as though you're over the marriage, but to fully recover after a significant loss, it's essential to grieve. A new relationship distracts you from this process. When we sabotage grief by denying it, replacing it, or attempting to skip grief stages, it resurfaces later in life and in the new marriage. As mentioned earlier, a minimum of two years should be taken to mourn the death of a marriage before dating. People who remarry within two years of their divorce have a much higher rate of a second divorce.

Second, and just as essential, the children aren't ready for a stepparent. Just as you need time to mourn, so do they. Your focus needs to be on helping your kids cope with the loss they've sustained. Adding a new marriage to the gamut of emotions will only prolong their healing.

Join a divorce-recovery support group and take time to heal before getting into a new relationship.

I believe I've learned from the mistakes I made in my first marriage and I'll know what not to do in the second one. Aren't mistakes the best teacher?

In a nutshell—no! The only thing we learn from making a mistake is that we make mistakes. Realizing that you were in error doesn't explain why you chose to act a certain way. The *why* is what points us toward restoration: Why is my anger out of control? Why do I think that way? What in my life has formed this behavior? Why do I make the same poor choices over and over?

Then after addressing the *why* questions, you must deal with *how*—how do I change this pattern? Breaking a destructive behavior takes much effort. You can't mix up a magic formula. Often, fixing surface issues doesn't get to the root of a problem. For instance, someone raised in an alcoholic home may be a rescuer. She may let people walk all over her, but being too nice isn't her real problem. Telling her to "become tougher and get some backbone" isn't going to work because it doesn't deal with how her past affected the way she sees and responds to others.

The first step is to find a counselor who can help you identify the root of the particular behavior you recognize as having caused strife in your marriage. Digging deeply and being open to learning about yourself is how you move toward recovery. Then you'll have learned from your mistakes!

My teenage son doesn't like my boyfriend even though he'd be a wonderful influence for him. How can I get my son to give this terrific guy a chance?

Children of all ages hold out hope that their parents will reunite. However, your son's response tells me he's also struggling with abandonment. The teen years are hard enough without added anger, fear, and loss. Your child needs you, not your new boyfriend, even if this man is the greatest. Your child senses the danger of losing you. He needs your undivided attention and listening ear. Even though he may push you away as if you were a leper, your role as the stable parent is to stay available. He wants and deserves the assurance that, after God, he's the highest priority in your life. He won't be persuaded with words but actions.

Try dating this man when your son is busy with friends or at his dad's place. If your son needs a healthy male influence, find a family at church where the dad is willing to pour time and compassion into your son's life. This is less intimidating to the boy because there's no threat of this man taking away his mother. This friend may be able to help ease your son's fears about someday having a stepdad.

Be careful not to make your son feel guilty because he isn't ready for your new relationship. And don't portray yourself as the martyr. In time, your son will mature and will feel more secure, and then you can attempt to reintroduce him to your boyfriend. It's a slow process that shouldn't be rushed.

I've met the most wonderful man who is everything my ex-husband wasn't. The chemistry with this new man makes me feel sexy and vibrant, and I fantasize about having sex with him. I know he feels the same way. My friends at church tell me it's wrong to have sex until we're married. But I don't believe God would want me to miss out on this pleasure. After all, God created sex, didn't He?

When my four-year-old grandson, Colin, comes to visit, the first place he heads toward is the fireplace. He's enamored by it. We've had several discussions about the fireplace, including how nice it is and the fact that it can be dangerous. He refuses to believe that if he sticks his hand near the pretty warm color it will hurt him. He sits back and waits for me to look the other way so he can put his hand on the protective screen.

I've had to instill some serious and painful consequences when his fingers cross the boundary line. Colin views me as cruel and unloving when I discipline him because he thinks I'm preventing him from having fun. Is that true? Am I intentionally tormenting my grandson by not allowing him to fulfill his desire? Would it be more loving of me to let him go near the fire? Of course not—that would be malicious, not loving. But that's exactly how we view God when He says no.

When God says no, it's for our good. When we don't understand God's motive for saying, "Don't touch," we'll see no reason to obey. Occasionally fear or guilt will stop us temporarily from doing something destructive, but eventually we rationalize that God will understand. And because the consequences aren't as swift as Colin's will be if he reaches into the flame, we convince ourselves that God is wrong to tell us no.

Pastor Kevin Myers of Crossroads Community Church in Lawrenceville, Georgia, says, "As soon as you learn that obedience is gold, it's never too heavy." In other words, once we understand that God's commands are a priceless treasure and keep us from injury, we will embrace them.

Did God create us as sexual beings? Yes. Is that a wonderful part of life? Yes. But sex is like the fire Colin wants to touch. In the fireplace it's a warm, comforting, glowing gift. But should a spark fly out and set the draperies aflame, it then becomes a catastrophe. In the same way, sex within marriage is delightful, but outside of marriage it causes decay. And the first relationship to disintegrate will be the most precious of all—the one with God.

Sometimes when my ex-husband picks up our six-year-old for visitation, my son will say something nice about my boyfriend or share a picture he drew for him at school. This makes my ex-husband furious and he lashes out at the child. How can I make my ex-husband stop doing this?

I don't advise introducing your child to the person you're dating until a marriage proposal is imminent. This prevents the child from suffering another loss should this relationship dissolve. If you and your

boyfriend are engaged, you can help defuse the situation. First, ask
God for the right words to speak to your ex-husband, and meet with
him when you can discuss things calmly without your son being present. Acknowledge his hurt over seeing the child respond to your
boyfriend. Compliment your ex on his parenting skills and reassure
him that your son will always love him and view him as his father.
Stress that you want to honor his relationship with your child and that
the boyfriend won't replace him. Help your ex see that his anger is
hurting his son and making him feel torn between the three of you.
Tell him you're open to suggestions on how you can all work to make
the situation a positive one for your son.

Here comes the hard part. To have this conversation, two things
must take place. First, you must truly mean what you are saying, and
second, you must be willing to listen to your ex-husband's point of
view. Ask God to help you see this situation from your ex-husband's
perspective and to reveal any areas where you unknowingly might be
sabotaging your child's relationship with his dad.

Unless there are abuse issues involved, your child's future and the
stability of your new marriage will be strengthened if your child has a
thriving relationship with his father as well as his stepdad.

Dear God,

*I feel both anxious and excited at the thought of a new romantic
relationship. I feel like an adolescent again. Sometimes the
thought of dating terrifies me, but the thought of being alone isn't
great either. I need Your wisdom, Lord. Reveal to me when my
heart is healed enough to date. Your Word says You'll guide me
with Your counsel and lead me to a glorious destiny. I want Your*

glorious destiny for my life, Lord. Your Word says no good thing will You withhold from those who walk with You.

Lord, as I begin the dating journey again, please help me to stay sexually pure. Your Word says You are faithful to help me be strong and that You guard me from evil. You created me, Lord, and You know everything about me, including my sexual desires. Help me to keep myself from situations that will tempt me to compromise Your beautiful gift of sex within marriage. Thank You for showing me that my worth isn't based on whether I have a date or a new relationship. You're all I need. Your Word explains that if I delight myself in You, You'll give me the desires of my heart. Thank You, Lord, for You know those desires before I even speak them.

(Portions of this prayer are taken from Psalm 37:4; 73:24; 84:11; and 2 Thessalonians 3:3.)

CHAPTER 10 QUESTIONS

1. What types of things can happen if someone jumps into the dating scene too quickly?
2. Do you agree that a separated or not-yet-divorced spouse should not date? Why, or why not?
3. In what ways can dating numb the heartache of divorce? Is this a good thing—or not? Why?
4. What effects can dating have on the children of the dating spouse?
5. How does 2 Corinthians 10:5 relate to dating?
6. What can we do if we feel like using people to make ourselves feel better or to project an image?

7. How can we know when we have fully grieved the loss of a pre-vious marriage—and are ready to date or even fall in love again? What happens if we skip part of the grieving process?

8. Is it possible for God to be all we need rather than depending on other people? Explain your answer.

9. What are some consequences of having sex outside of marriage? Why does God say this is wrong? What are the potential conse-quences for you and your children if you don't remain sexually pure?

To Do This Week ...

- Write down all the things that were the "red flags" when dating your former spouse. Did you ignore them?

- After attending a divorce-recovery support group, find a seminar or group that helps to explain what to look for when dating.

11

Help! I'm Over 50

DIVORCING LATER IN LIFE

Age does not diminish the extreme disappointment of having a scoop of ice cream fall from the cone.

JIM FIEBIG

Talk to almost any experienced divorce-recovery facilitator and he or she will tell you one of the most significant trends over the last few years is the increase in the age of those attending workshops, as well as the number of years they were married.

Empty-nest experts Sheri and Bob Stritof share this information on www.About.com:

> The sad news is that there has been a steady increase in the number of divorces among couples married 30 or more years. Many long-term married couples divorce one another after the kids leave home. They realize too late that their children kept them together. Other couples divorce during the empty nest years because they can't handle the health issues and the sense of an uncertain future along with being overwhelmed by too much togetherness.

On September 20, 2007, the *New York Times* posted an article authored by Sam Roberts that substantiates their opinion. "Don't stock up on silver anniversary cards. More than half the Americans who might have celebrated their 25th wedding anniversary since 2000 were divorced, separated or widowed before reaching that milestone, according to the latest census survey." He continues, "For the first time at least since World War II, women and men who married in the late 1970s had less than even a chance of still being married 25 years later."

Here are a few reasons why this trend is occurring:

- People are living longer.
- People in this age group have a more carefree attitude about money, debt, and spending than in previous generations.
- Many baby boomers abandoned the traditional church as young adults. Some returned for a season when their kids were young, but found the church irrelevant for themselves. So they left again, and now they have little attachment or reverence for God, or His standards for marriage.
- When their kids were young, couples ignored numerous significant issues that were harming the marriage. Now the kids are grown, and they feel like strangers.
- They possess a "Life is short and then you die" mentality.
- They embrace an "I deserve to be happy no matter what" frame of mind.
- Society has become more transient. This results in less connection to the children and grandchildren, which makes it easier to walk away from the spouse and family.
- Retirement often places the couple under the same roof day

and night. One or both parties may feel as though they are suffocating.

I've devoted this entire chapter to those who separated or divorced later in life, often after many years of marriage. The following situations come directly from people over fifty who have shared their stories, questions, or concerns.

Keep in mind that other chapters in this book may contain the information older readers are seeking on a specific topic, such as finances or forgiveness.

I married as a teenager and now at fifty-five I find myself single again after a divorce. I've been part of a couple almost my whole life. The loneliness is overwhelming, and I'm not certain how to cope.

Healthy, stable, same-sex friends are the key to surviving loneliness after divorce. God created us for community. We were never designed to go though life alone. Often the initial response after a devastating loss is to isolate ourselves. But it's at this time when we need people more than ever.

When we share, give, and experience life with others, we find meaning again.

One person took life's lemons and made lemonade this way: "Even though I did not want a divorce, I've decided to make the best of it. I married very young, and never really experienced being single. Therefore, I've decided this is a wonderful opportunity to become single for the first time. I love my friends; they have been extremely supportive and helpful."

Once your grief begins to subside, consider volunteering to help others. One group that would welcome you with open arms is divorce recovery for kids. It's a wonderful and rewarding place to serve. Children often lose their grandparents during a divorce and they desperately need an older person to fill the gap of that loss.

As you become emotionally stronger, use your pain to help others. I love to remind the devil that the devastation he intended to destroy me has served to make me more fervent to help those who are hurting. This brings purpose to my pain and allows me to spit in the eye of evil.

In our marriage of thirty years my husband was selfish, immature, and money-centered. I was a world-class nag, immature, and depressed. Although we tried counseling before ending the marriage, I now realize we had been divorced in our hearts for years. What could we have done differently?

When you put two people under the same roof for a period of time, problems are likely to arise. That's because our self-centered natures eventually show their ugly faces. Our society doesn't recognize this. We have convinced ourselves that the human race is basically good. However, if we are honest and seek God's Word on this subject we discover that our initial response in many circumstances is self-serving. A small child's behavior easily validates this point. Without being taught, a child will instinctively grab a toy from another child—even hitting if necessary—and say "mine." No one teaches children to be disobedient or nasty. It comes naturally.

Egotistic thinking doesn't automatically go away when we become adults. It often morphs into other behaviors such as cruel words and malicious conduct. The more hurt a person experienced during childhood and the growing- up years, the more likely he or she is to inflict that pain onto others. This is why it's crucial for people to deal with past emotional wounds.

If we surrender our lives to Christ and ask to become like Him, a kinder, more mature nature can develop. When both people in a marriage allow Christ to mold them into someone who loves as He loves, healing can begin and harmony often follows.

I'm sorry your marriage ended. If neither of you have remarried, I encourage you to consider discussing what I have shared. It's never too late to ask Christ to heal a broken relationship.

My wife of thirty years and I often talked about all the things we would do in our retirement years. But last year she started spending a lot of her time with new friends. Now she wants a divorce. What happened?

Without speaking to your wife, this is difficult to answer. My immediate response is that one of four things may have occurred.

First, she is in a new relationship and doesn't want to hurt you by sharing the truth. Second, she was very unhappy in the marriage all along but didn't express her true feelings. Third, she was miserable and did share her feelings but you didn't understand how serious it was. Fourth, her age has caused her to calculate how many years she might have left and she has concluded that it's wise to "live what's left of life to the full." For some of today's seniors that translates into dumping a spouse, kids, grandkids, and all responsibility.

I don't know which of these applies to your circumstance. Share these thoughts with her and ask for honesty. Once you understand why she desires a divorce it will be easier to process the loss.

I'm truly sorry for your pain. I know firsthand how hard it is to endure a divorce. I encourage you to join a divorce-recovery support group. This will provide much-needed comfort and friendships.

> **After twenty-seven years of marriage my husband and I are separated. However, he wants to remain friends and have fun. We are sexually intimate and share numerous activities together. I love him and can't imagine my life without him, but I don't know how long I can continue the relationship in this manner. I cry all the time when we are apart. He refuses to discuss reconciliation, and I suspect there are other women in his life.**

It sounds as though you are living the life of a mistress, not a wife. Your fear of losing this man is holding you hostage, and that apprehension is causing you to make choices that are not wise. I understand how easy it is to think remaining intimate may restore your marriage, but if you look deeply you'll see otherwise.

Sexual intimacy should be reserved for a married couple that is committed to each other. The faithfulness and security of knowing that this precious union is not shared with anyone else is part of what makes the act sacred and beautiful. It's also what makes a woman feel safe and secure. In this relationship you have none of those things.

Your husband is using you for his sexual pleasure and for the familiarity of your twenty-seven years of companionship. This is not marriage, and it is not healthy. Relationships are built on love, trust, commitment and respect. If your spouse respected you, he would desire that you feel validated and special, not merely one of his many girls. Lack of respect causes someone to treat another person worse, not better. This behavior doesn't restore a relationship but destroys it. Because you are God's precious daughter He doesn't want you treated this way.

This is going to be hard to hear. If you are correct about the other women in his life, you are exposing yourself to sexually transmitted diseases. I strongly suggest that you see a gynecologist to be tested. Advertisements for medical treatment of these diseases often display younger people. This leaves older men and women with the misconception that it's unlikely they will contract one. However, I assure you these diseases know no age, gender, or race. It can happen to you. Therefore, I advise you to see your doctor as quickly as possible.

It's time to take a long look at where this relationship is headed and decide what you want from life. I suggest setting healthy boundaries that will point this marriage in the direction of a loving commitment. When he stops receiving free sex and companionship with no commitments, he will either step out of the relationship or work on building the trust and marriage again. If he leaves for good, keep your eyes on Christ and eventually you will heal.

When my husband's father died three years ago his whole personality changed. Once a loving husband and father, he became depressed and withdrawn. Now he wants a divorce. I don't understand any of this. He is sixty-eight years old and wasn't even close to his dad.

One of the surprising things I have encountered while talking to men and women who divorce later in life is that the death of a family member—in particular a parent—was what triggered the decision to walk out of the marriage.

Counselors say the death of a parent highlights our own mortality. When we realize we won't live forever, some people respond by thinking, "I'd better get out there and see what I've been missing."

If the relationship included painful issues from the past, a parent's death may expose unresolved anger. The opportunity to confront them is gone forever, and the mounting frustration can activate a variety of responses.

Whatever the reason, when a person has a drastic change in personality it's a good idea to see a medical doctor and possibly a counselor. If you can persuade your husband to see either of these professionals it might help salvage your marriage. If he refuses, there isn't much you can do. Pray for him. It appears he is deeply hurting.

For thirty-plus years the "other woman" in my life has been my mother-in-law. She has hated me my entire married life. Therefore, when my husband decided to walk out, it was no surprise that he moved in with his "mommy." I'm so angry with her I don't know what to do.

Mother-in-law jokes have been around for a long time, and sometimes with good reason. As a stepmother of adult boys, I'm now a mother-in-law myself, so I'm aware of just how strong the temptation to meddle can be. However, I've met a number of women who truly can't let go of their precious baby even if he or she is six feet tall.

Coping with anger is a natural part of divorce. It's not, "Will I get angry?" as much as, "What do I do with all this anger?" Anger itself is not wrong. It's how we act out the emotion that causes negative consequences. If we let anger brew inside, it turns into bitterness, resentment, and even depression. And that's a dangerous trio.

Seek to understand why you are angry. Are you mad at him for leaving you? Are you resentful toward his mother for treating you badly? Are you furious with yourself for putting up with it? Do you blame his mother for the divorce? Is there something else lurking below the obvious? Once you walk through what is making you upset, it will be easier to lay that feeling down.

Releasing anger is similar to letting go of resentment and choosing forgiveness. It's a choice and a process. Sometimes we have to do it over and over if the person continues to hurt us.

Ask God to help you see your mother-in-law through God's eyes. It's amazing what God reveals when we sincerely ask for His perspective.

After twenty-eight years my marriage ended in divorce. I lost my health insurance and retirement funds in the process. I am not eligible for group health insurance. I never imagined I'd be without coverage at this stage of my life.

Health insurance can be one of the biggest unexpected losses during divorce. Even if you were involved in paying the bills before the divorce, a huge shock can arise when you realize how much this will cost. One woman shared with me, "While we were married I did all the financial stuff and bill-paying for our household. However, I was shocked at the expenses I needed to pick up after the divorce that had previously been covered by my husband's employer."

Health insurance issues are of major concern to many people right now. You have a number of options and your doctor's office may have suggestions. I looked into AARP (www.AARP.org) and Medishare (www.Medishare.org) when I was seeking private insurance. They provided me with excellent information.

Retirement funds are another area of concern. My suggestion is to ask your church leaders if they know a volunteer budget counselor or financial planner who might be willing to sit down with you and explain your options. Do a little research and find out if he or she is reputable. Be careful that the person isn't trying to sell you something. This should only be advice at this point. If you need to make investments, hire a certified financial planner.

I have a medical condition that will progressively get worse as I age. I thought my husband of twenty-eight years would be around to take care of me, but he left. I have children, but they live in another state. I'm truly at a loss.

Of all the scenarios I face in divorce recovery, this one troubles me the most. At a time in life when an illness is attacking you physically, emotionally, and possibly even causing your faith to wane, the person who was supposed to stand by you "in sickness and in health" walks out. I don't understand this behavior.

The good news is that God hasn't walked out on you. When people abandon us it's reassuring to know God is steadfast, our ever-present anchor. In John 14:18 Jesus tells us, "I will not leave you as orphans; I will come to you." And in Jeremiah 49:11 God specifically addresses the widow's plight (which is what you are), "Leave your orphans; I will protect their lives. Your widows too can trust in me."

It is dangerous to put our trust and hope in people. They sometimes disappoint us. But God will not discard you. He will provide. Often His method of doing that is through the body of Christ. If your

church does not have a support system for people going through difficult life circumstances I suggest you research other churches in your
area that do. You need help; don't be embarrassed or ashamed to ask.
That's one of the main purposes for the church and community.

Your doctor's office may also be of assistance. Often they know of
groups that address specific illnesses. Ask the nurse or receptionist for
resources. And don't give up. You are beautiful in God's eyes.

**My spouse was very controlling and never allowed me to be part
of any decisions. After many years of marriage, he left me. I'm
on my own and terrified. He often told me I was stupid and I
think he was right because I'm afraid to make small purchases,
much less big ones. What am I going to do?**

Let's get one thing perfectly clear: You are not stupid. The fact that
you knew to ask for help proves it. When we repeatedly hear demean-
ing and cruel remarks about ourselves, we often begin to take on that
identity. Just because your husband said this about you doesn't make it
true. Let's look at what God's Word says in Isaiah 43:3-4, "For I am
the LORD, your God, the Holy One of Israel, your Savior.... Since you
are precious and honored in my sight, and because I love you." You are
valued and loved by God. You are His beloved.

Step-by-step you can learn to do all the things required to maintain a household. My guess is that you have friends and can find
people at your church who would be willing to help you through the
process. Tell leaders of a divorce-recovery program about your needs.
It's not wrong or a sign of weakness to ask for help.

One woman took this step. "I remember when I had to buy my
first car without my husband, I asked an elder in my church to go

along because my stomach was in knots and I was full of anxiety. I was afraid to make decisions because I was certain they would be wrong, and that I (or others) would have to suffer the consequences of my decisions." She was still afraid, but she walked toward the fear by asking another person for assistance.

Note: If you decide to ask a male friend for help and he is married, include his wife. This prevents jealousy or temptation toward anything inappropriate. You are vulnerable right now, and it would be easy to view any kind man as a "knight in shining armor" coming to rescue you. God is your rescuer, no one else.

After I endured thirty-two years of tolerating an unfaithful husband, my spouse decided to walk out and divorce me. I assumed that if I stood by him during his wandering years, I'd have a husband and a marriage as we got older. I'm the one who was faithful, but I'm the one who has ended up alone. This isn't fair.

Fair is a word that typically doesn't come into play very much during divorce. Often one person bears the brunt of the other's poor choices. Learning how to forgive can be painfully difficult, but it's not impossible.

Sadly, your former spouse decided to live in betrayal of his marriage. He obviously has been deceived into believing that God "looks the other way" when we disobey Him. Is it possible he came to this conclusion because you decided to "look the other way"? He never faced consequences for his sinful behavior or the pain that might have caused him to repent. Therefore he sank more deeply into his problem.

I am not implying that you caused him to sin. That decision was his own foolish choice. What I am saying is that by allowing it to continue without consequences, you became part of the problem. You withheld from him the very thing that might have forced him to wake up and turn around.

Find a support group that helps people understand the difference between leniency and love. God will reveal this truth if you seek Him. Jeremiah 33:3 gives us this assurance, "Call to me and I will answer you and tell you great and unsearchable things you do not know."

After thirty-one years of marriage I find myself divorced. I feel like I'm losing my mind. I expected my adult kids and grandkids to stand by me but they don't seem to comprehend my pain. Don't they see my tears?

You aren't losing your mind. It's merely that we often expect the people closest to us to grasp the depth of our pain, and frequently they can't or won't. This causes frustration and hurt.

It's also possible that you want your kids to take your side in the divorce and this makes them uncomfortable. Subtly you may be communicating that if they remain close to the other parent and refuse to turn against him or her, they're rejection you or slapping you in the face.

Ponder the following questions. Be honest with yourself. Are you giving your family permission to love the other parent? Do you view time spent with him or her as a betrayal to you? Are you attempting to manipulate your family with gifts, guilt, or tears? Are you looking to family to heal the hurt in your heart? Are you expecting them to fill your calendar and keep you busy? If so, this is placing a tremendous and unrealistic burden on them.

I understand that these questions are blunt and may sting emotionally. It's normal to want our families nearby in times of crisis. Having a close relationship is a good thing. However, when we look to family or friends to meet all of our needs, relationships become unhealthy. We are expecting people to give what only God can provide. If you are having a hard time with all of this, an objective third party can provide a fresh perspective.

I'm in my late sixties and it's been two years since my second divorce from a twenty-two-year marriage. I thought I'd be over it by now. But I'm not. What's wrong with me?

Society and Hollywood portray divorce as a common occurrence, void of negative emotions and trauma. They are wrong. But when we experience the pain and loss of divorce we are astonished. It's the death of a relationship and a major loss. Grieving takes time. The fact that this was a second divorce makes the process more difficult. When a second marriage ends it affects our faith in the institution of marriage. This can kill the dream of finding the "perfect" relationship.

If the main objective after a divorce is to get over it, that reveals a bigger problem, a misunderstanding about marriage and relationships. A better goal after divorce would be to discover, "How did I end up here?" This will require digging past the obvious problems such as stepchildren, affairs, addictions, etc.—and exploring the deeper issues.

The chapter in this book entitled, "How Did I Get Here?" can provide you with more help on this topic. Professional assistance from a Christian counselor or therapist can also give you insights into why you've divorced again.

I just heard that my former spouse of twenty-eight years is getting remarried. I didn't think such news would bother me, but I'm very upset and I can't stop thinking about it.

It's interesting how a former spouse getting married or having a baby can trigger nostalgia or sad emotions. This is often true even if you wanted the marriage to end. It may be because the information reminds us that we were once joined together in a one-flesh union—now it's over. It's also not uncommon to experience a strange realization such as, "I was once married to that person and now I hardly know him or her." I've had this happen to me, and it's a bizarre moment that's hard to explain unless you have experienced it. I've had others share with me that after a divorce they too have wondered why they have similar thoughts. I think it's because marriage wasn't supposed to be temporary. It's a union that's a mystery and something only God fully comprehends.

If the former spouse walked out, the new relationship may make us feel defective or inadequate all over again. If the new love interest is younger or more attractive, that can be a severe blow to our self-worth.

Pray and ask God to reveal why these emotions are resurfacing. He may reveal unresolved issues that need to be addressed.

Note the wedding date and make plans immediately. Have something fun with a friend scheduled for the whole day. Don't sit around the house moping or brooding. Do not ask the adult children questions about the occasion. This puts them in an awkward position.

Consider something that may help you feel better physically too. One lady had a great suggestion: "During my divorce I sought out a massage therapist. This was an amazing help as I missed human touch, and I could just cry and let myself relax." Ahhh. Doesn't that sound wonderful?

Dear Lord,

This gut-wrenching experience is causing my heart to ache as much as my joints. I used to wonder if death would take my spouse from me, but I never dreamed my soul mate would walk out. When we got married and had a family, I assumed we would grow elderly together. But now I feel old, poor, alone, and afraid.

Your Word tells me that You love me with an everlasting love and I desire to believe it's true. It also says when I get old, You will take care of me and provide for my needs. I want to trust You, Lord, because my human resources are depleted. There is no spouse left to lean on. You are my only hope. Give me the strength and courage I need to live victoriously.

Teach me to be a godly example to my children. Remind me often that even though they are adults, they are also confused and hurting. I pray You will protect my grandchildren from the effects of this divorce. Help them to overcome any wounds this has caused in their lives.

I give it all to You, God. You are the only one big enough for this problem. I look to You as my strength and my redeemer.

(Portions of this prayer are taken from Jeremiah 31:3; Isaiah 46:4; and Job 19:25.)

Chapter 11 Questions

1. The author shares several reasons why the divorce rate is on the

rise among people over age fifty. Does your situation fall into any of these categories? Why do you think people in this age range are divorcing more frequently?

2. What are some of the issues that are unique to a person divorcing later in life? What would you tell others in your age range who are considering divorce?

3. Did this separation or divorce take you by surprise, or did you somewhat suspect it might happen?

4. Often adult children can struggle as much as younger kids when parents divorce. How are your children handling the situation?

5. How has your divorce affected your relationship with the grandchildren? Do they ask difficult questions that are hard to answer? Have you researched where to find help for them?

6. Sometimes old friends disappear during divorce. How are friends responding to your circumstances? Do you have a strong support system?

7. What financial concerns are you attempting to overcome during the divorce?

8. What does "living life to the full" mean to you? How do you plan on doing that now that you are divorced?

To Do This Week ...

- If you are a senior, reach out to a child in your church or neighborhood who has lost contact with a grandparent because of a death or divorce.

12

I'm Back in Court—Again!!

Until you do an autopsy on your last marriage, you are
bringing the dead body into the next one.

DR. PHIL MCGRAW

The sitcom *The Brady Bunch* ran on television from 1969–1974 and still shows up on cable channels. A teenager at the time, I thought Greg Brady was the handsomest thing I ever saw.

Wikipedia describes *The Brady Bunch* this way: "Despite its less than stellar primetime ratings and having won no awards, the show has become a true cultural phenomenon, having lasted in the minds of Americans and in syndication for over 35 years."

It continues:

> Mike Brady, a widowed architect with sons Greg, Peter and
> Bobby, married Carol Martin (née Tyler), whose daughters
> were Marcia, Jan and Cindy. The daughters took the Brady
> surname. Sherwood Schwartz, creator of the series, wanted
> Carol to have been a divorcée. The network objected to
> this, but a compromise was reached whereby no mention

was made of the circumstances in which Carol's first marriage ended, but many assume she was widowed.

What I remember most was that almost everyone on the show was cute, polite, and respectful. A perky attitude was maintained no matter what the circumstances. On the rare occasion when the family did have a conflict they always resolved the problem and concluded with sweet apologies and warm hugs for everyone. And all of this mending occurred within thirty minutes. Amazing! Aside from Florence Henderson's hairdo, the show had just one problem: The whole situation was pathetically unrealistic. Think about it—What could possibly go wrong with a family that has a full-time housekeeper?

The audience never heard Greg scream at Cindy, "I hate you and I wish you didn't live here. We had our dad (and the bathroom) all to ourselves before you came along." Nor did we observe a weeping Marcia banter, "You aren't my real dad. Don't tell me what to do." And Mike never said to Carol, "You are putting me in the middle again. Don't make me choose between you and my kids."

However, ask those who are familiar with stepfamily living and most will exclaim that those comments are very typical. The stress and obstacles they encounter are much more complicated and multi-faceted than they could have predicted.

Wait a minute. Shouldn't a second marriage be easier than the first one? Doesn't a person learn how to "do marriage" better after one has failed? In most cases the answer is no. And the causes are numerous. The first reason is that many people neglect to find out the true under-lying problems that caused the divorce. They blame the affair or addiction but never discovered the root reasons. If the person never went through divorce recovery or counseling, chances are they never got down to deeper issues that caused the demise of the relationship. Therefore, the chances of a second marriage following the same bad pattern increased. E. Mavis Hetherington, principal researcher of the Virginia Longitudinal Study of Divorce and Remarriage and author of the book *For Better or For Worse*, confirmed that the overall divorce rate for stepcouples in her study was between 65 and 70 percent. Furthermore, because not all stepfamilies have the same level of complexity, Hetherington went on to specify that "simple stepfamilies" (where only one partner brought a child or children to the new marriage) divorced at a rate of 65 percent; when both partners had children from previous relationships ("complex stepfamilies") the divorce rate was slightly more than 70 percent. By the year 2010 it is predicted that there will be more stepfamilies in America than any other type of family (single parent or traditional first-marriage).[1]

A second reason that repeat marriages fail centers on the presence of children from a previous marriage. In a child's mind he is losing a parent, not gaining a new one. That fear is a powerful force. I remember my six-year-old nephew, Ian, crying at his mother's second wedding. With his head buried in her white gown he clung to her leg begging, "Mommy, please stay plain. Please stay plain." It was his way of saying, "I don't like this change."

A study on stepfamilies reveals that kids view remarriage of their parents differently than adults.

> Children and adults often define family membership differently. In one study, children and adults were asked to identify people they consider their family. Less than 10% of children failed to mention a biological parent, but 31% did not include a residential stepparent in their

family list. They were also more likely to omit stepsiblings from the list (41%). Just 15% of adults, on the other hand, neglected to list stepchildren.[2]

Therefore, kids consciously or not often set out to sabotage the relationship in order to regain the parent they believe they have lost. And many times they succeed.

I know firsthand that this is true. When I married my present husband twenty-two years ago, he had two boys, age eleven and fourteen. Because I remarried much too quickly and hadn't fully healed from the wounds of my first marriage, I only understood how difficult the transition was for me. But now, after many years in divorce-recovery ministry, I realize how much worse it was for his sons.

During the eight years before I came along, his boys spent a lot of time with their dad even though they lived with their mom. Then one day it happened. Ta-da!—the Wicked Stepmother arrives on the scene. Suddenly they no longer have Dad all to themselves. This new wife requested that they sit at the table and eat turkey and mashed potatoes during Sunday dinner. The former routine was to eat pizza in front of the TV and toss the box under the couch. Everything changed for them when I came along and the resentment and anger mounted.

They are grown adults now with kids of their own. We have a good relationship, but I wish I had more fully understood how to transition into a stepfamily. Not as many resources were available to stepfamilies back then as there are now, but if we had researched information from those who understood the challenges associated with remarriage it might have helped. We blindly and foolishly assumed the boys would adjust. The stress often caused problems in our marriage.

We stayed together, but I know many couples with stepchildren do not. The only reason our marriage has survived for twenty-two years is because I got professional help. Counseling revealed the wounds of my childhood and teen years, as well as the grief I was still carrying from my first marriage. I discovered how those destructive patterns and scars were affecting my present attitude, decisions, and marriage. I also learned that the pain of my childhood created a distorted view of God that kept me from accepting Him as a faithful, warm Daddy who longed to lavish me with love. Although I accepted Jesus as my Savior as a young adult, fear and a lack of trust kept Him at arm's length and away from my heart. This warped view of God was affecting every area of my life, and it was time to replace the lies with truth.

Stepfamily issues are complex so not every circumstance can be addressed in this chapter. For more information on stepfamilies and kids I've included a list of great resources in the back of this book. For a live seminar I recommend Ron Deal's *Building A Successful Stepfamily*. He does an excellent job of explaining the various issues associated with remarriage.

For individual counseling I recommend seeing someone who specializes in your areas of need. Start by asking your church if they have a name, but if they suggest a non-professional or a counselor who has no experience with stepfamily issues then I would look elsewhere for a referral. Many people do not comprehend the extremely difficult issues associated with divorce, which typically need more assistance than a volunteer or inexperienced person can provide. Larger churches usually have a list of counselors that they recommend. Remember that pastors have a full plate of commitments and often do not have the time or experience to deal with intense problems. Do not assume that a pastor can or should help you past encouragement and prayer.

Now let's explore answers to some of the difficult questions that arise when a second or third marriage ends in divorce.

❀❀❀

I can't believe this is happening to me again, but I am going through my second divorce. We dated for three years before getting remarried in an effort to be certain that we were right for each other. What happened?

It's common for a person to think that dating for a considerable amount of time before remarriage guarantees marital success, but that's no truer for a second marriage than the first time around.

The faulty thinking is rooted in the belief that a successful marriage is about finding the right person. But the first step to having a good marriage is becoming a stable, emotionally healthy person who makes wise choices. Each person needs to discover what is wounded or broken in his or her own heart and work to heal those areas before moving into a relationship. Sometimes this can be very painful at first. But in the end it's worth it.

When you do that you will become much better at finding others who are making wise choices.

I thought for sure "the third time is a charm" would be true for my marriage. But I'm divorcing again. How long should I wait to begin dating again?

My suggestion would be that you put dating completely out of your mind. The fact that you have experienced three divorces is an indication that something is broken in your ability to maintain healthy relationships.

The first thing I recommend is to find a divorce-recovery support group in your area. Second, find an objective and honest same-sex friend at your church who can provide good judgment. Sit down with your friend and say, "I'm giving you permission to speak the truth in love to me. What am I doing wrong in my relationships?"

Often when someone is not emotionally involved in our circumstances they can provide a sensible perspective that we cannot see on our own. However, you'll want to pick an emotionally healthy person who is discerning and has some understanding of why relationships fail. Sometimes a divorce-recovery facilitator or marriage mentor is good at sharing these insights.

I believed it was impossible to feel worse than I did during my first divorce. However, the feelings of failure that I'm experiencing during my second divorce are ten times worse than before. I did not want this. Why am I overwhelmed with guilt and shame?

Divorce almost always produces a sense of loss and devastation. In an attempt to soothe the pain we convince ourselves that the next time will be better. When it isn't better, we feel a real blow to our self-worth and belief system.

We spend a large amount of mental exhaustion wondering what others are thinking about us. Our mind races with thoughts such as, "Now that this has happened to me twice will people automatically think I'm a horrible spouse?" or "What's wrong with me? Am I incapable of holding on to a mate?" This is the time to learn how to deal with these thoughts and discover the truth.

If your identity is attached to your marital status, that's the first place to start. If your value is associated with marriage or a romantic relationship, that's a problem. Our identity needs to come from the fact that we have a Creator who loves us just because He made us. When I look elsewhere to find my purpose in life it leads to frustration and loss. If this information is new to you or difficult to understand, please contact someone at your church for help.

My second suggestion is to find a counselor who can help you discover the patterns and common denominators between the two marriages. Initially this may be painful, but it's crucial for complete healing.

> **My first husband kept his addiction to drugs well hidden, I thought my second husband was a social drinker but as it turns out he was an alcoholic. Now I'm on my third divorce, and this man has a sexual addiction and abused my kids. Why do I keep marrying the wrong man?**

The root of this problem is not that you keep picking the wrong man. The need in you that these men were meeting is the underlying issue that must be uncovered in order for the pattern to cease. If these chaotic, destructive relationships didn't meet a need in you, you wouldn't keep repeating the same pattern.

Why do you gravitate to people who have destructive addictions? Shift your thinking from discovering why you pick the wrong men to "What is broken in me that I repeatedly choose people who are toxic?" When you discover the answer to that question you will be on the road to healing.

I recommend a Celebrate Recovery group. (See Resources section.)

They specialize in helping people break free from destructive patterns and choices.

My second marriage ended after seven years. I was certain my second husband would stay close with the kids from my first marriage, but he hasn't made any effort to see them at all. How could he stop loving them overnight?

If this man has been good to your children in the past, don't assume that he has stopped loving them. It may be too painful for him to see them, or he may not be sure how you or the biological father feels about him staying in their lives. Some stepparents decide to cut all ties with the children because it's a reminder of what has been lost, or they want to move on to a new relationship without the attachment of the kids. There are a variety of reasons why this occurs.

It's best to sit down with your second husband in a calm, non-accusatory setting and ask him why he isn't staying in touch with the kids. Explain that they would like to see him, and share the reasons why you think it would be good for them to maintain a relationship. Assure him that this is for the children and that you are not using them to continue to have a relationship with him yourself.

His response will tell you what to do next. Either you will set up a visitation schedule, or he will walk away. If he refuses to respond, then you have your answer. It will then be your responsibility to help the children understand that it's not their fault. They are suffering a loss, and although church support systems should help, remember they also need you to you remain a constant source of reinforcement.

I plead with you to resist the thinking that what they need is a new daddy. The worst thing you could do is to introduce a new man into their world. To a child this subconsciously communicates another threat: the loss of you. You are the one person who should always be there for them.

I have two sons, ages twelve and fifteen, who are ecstatic that I divorced their stepdad of eight years. I thought kids hated divorce. Why are they so glad I've gone through a second divorce?

James Dobson in his book *Bringing Up Boys* sheds insight on what happens to children when a mom remarries: "The research confirms that remarriage of a parent makes things worse for boys. The odds for youths in stepparent families are similar to those who do not live with any parents. Apparently stepfathers and children frequently compete for the time, attention, and resources of the biological mother, creating conflict and bitterness."[3]

However that doesn't mean your second divorce has not affected your sons. "Even if the kids hate the stepparent, they will go through a re-grieving process when the second marriage breaks up," said divorce-recovery expert Tom Whiteman. His advice reveals that even if your kids appear to be happy and relieved, they still experience some level of grief. It's another loss. I suggest taking them to a counselor who specializes in teens because the effect of a second divorce on kids is profound.

When I married my former wife, she was a single parent with a three-year-old daughter. After seven years of marriage, this child now feels like my own and I love her dearly. However, her mother will not let me see her anymore. She says I'm not the biological father so I have no rights. I'm heartbroken and don't know what to do.

I am so sorry for your situation; this has been a terrible loss for you and your stepdaughter. Many people become attached to their stepchildren, and it often feels like a death when they lose them during divorce.

Unfortunately, the simple truth is that unless your former wife decides to let you visit with her daughter, you probably will have no relationship until the child is old enough to decide on her own.

You could consider obtaining legal advice, but in most states the law won't help. Another option is to explain your situation to an objective person that the mom trusts. This person may be able to help her to see the child's perspective, and that time with you would be beneficial for her healing.

If she refuses, then all you can do is accept her decision and pray for the child. If she will allow you to send birthday cards or gifts this will help the child to know she has not been forgotten.

When I got remarried eight years ago, I had two young girls from my first marriage. Shortly after our wedding we moved several states away from my children's biological dad. Even though we planned a regular visitation schedule, over time the kids saw him less and less. Now that I'm divorcing a second time, my oldest daughter constantly screams at me, "You took me away from my own father for a marriage that didn't even last." She is really angry with me and I feel guilty.

Children who remain in close contact with both biological parents do much better than the ones who have little or no contact. Therefore, kids should not be moved away from a parent unless it absolutely cannot be avoided. This is true even if it means the stepparent must turn down a better job opportunity. The only exception is if the children are in danger when visiting a parent.

When parents remarry it is absolutely crucial that the emotional stability of the kids remains the highest priority. The problem comes when a parent believes it won't harm the child to be taken away from the biological parent and that the stepparent can fill the void.

As you experienced when one parent lives far away, the visitation schedule often falls through even if a good plan is in place. And now your child is resentful and angry that she has been cheated out of time with her father.

My suggestion is for you to contact the father and discuss the situation and explain that you now realize it was a mistake. Then I'd make an appointment with a good Christian counselor who understands children and divorce. Your younger daughter should attend also because she may be internalizing emotions and not expressing them outwardly.

My kids didn't know their dad very much; he left when they were young. They became attached to my second husband and now we are divorcing. They seem very upset and I don't know what to do.

Younger kids who do not have one of their biological parents in their lives often bond with the stepparent. The *Successful Stepfamily* Web site shares:

> When the co-parental relationship between ex-spouses has "dissolved" because one biological parent is no longer emotionally involved with the children, the stepparent's role is generally enhanced. Stepparents find it easier to

emotionally bond with stepchildren who are thirsty for another adult in their life.

I must also add that you would be making a huge mistake to intentionally try to eliminate the biological parent from a child's life in order to force the bond with a stepparent. The article continues, "Custodial parents should not, however, try to alienate their children from the other biological parent in order to make the insertion of a stepparent easier. That only backfires and creates resentment throughout the two homes."[4]

Your children are experiencing the loss of the only real dad they have ever known, except their pain is even worse. Their biological father has walked away and now they are losing a second father, producing a double rejection.

The information I have written in chapter 4 about kids and divorce applies to your daughters. If your ex-husband is willing to maintain a relationship with the girls and attend counseling with them, it will help immensely.

I suggest finding a kids' divorce-recovery program at a nearby church as soon as possible. This will help them cope with the various emotions they are enduring.

After only three years of marriage I'm divorced again. Although the feeling of failure is horrible, I'm relieved to be away from the tension of the stepchildren. I feel guilty that I'm glad to be rid of them. Is this normal?

Any time stress is reduced in our life, feelings of relief are natural. And the turmoil that surrounds stepfamilies is often much worse than people realize. When my stepsons were younger, there were days that I wanted to run from the whole mess. I felt like a failure because it seemed I was always doing or saying the wrong thing. And I couldn't talk to my husband about it because these were his kids and I didn't want to do something hurtful.

Although most people would not admit it, I know many who struggle to like—much less love—their stepchildren. It takes time and sometimes professional help.

I'd suggest that you take a long look at the relationship and discover what went wrong. Did you properly prepare for the complex issues associated with stepfamilies? Did you believe that because you and your spouse were in love that the kids would automatically follow along? These and many other circumstances are the reasons second marriages fail.

My husband's ex-wife was the main source of stress in our marriage. She constantly caused problems over financial issues and visitation with the kids. Although I'm upset that the marriage is over, I'm glad to be rid of her. Why didn't we realize it was going to be so difficult?

Even when warned about the difficulty of stepfamilies, most engaged couples convince themselves that their situation will be different. They so desperately long to become like a "normal" family again that they ignore the pressures associated with second marriage.

This denial ultimately leads to family struggles. The stepfamilies who survive are the ones who realistically look at the issues and get help. They admit that bringing two families together is going to be a lot of work, and they research books, seminars, and leaders who understand.

A former spouse is often one of the most constant sources of tension because he or she is the biological parent. If this person is unstable, unreasonable, or self-centered it can cause tremendous stress on the marriage.

My kids want to see their stepdad even though he and I are divorcing. My first husband is furious that his biological children still desire a relationship with their stepfather. I'm so confused.

This is a difficult situation, and the only thing you can do is sit down with the biological dad and have a talk. Listen carefully and let him explain why he objects to them having a relationship with the stepdad. Chances are that he feels threatened by the relationship and is concerned that the kids will feel closer to the stepdad than they do to him.

Calmly explain to him that this isn't about the kids loving him any less, but rather the grief they are feeling. It may help to have him talk to someone who leads a divorce-recovery program for kids. An objective third party may be able to explain the layers of loss children experience when someone they care for is no longer around and the fact that the children may resent him later for preventing the relationship. If he is a reasonable man who truly loves his kids, he will eventually understand that it's in the best interest of the kids for them to remain in contact with their stepfather. Once he understands that this is not about him losing his children but rather them coping with their grief, it should help.

My first husband is getting divorced from his second wife. They have a child together and my seven-year-old biological daughter is very close to her half sister. She doesn't understand why the relationship is changing.

My heart aches for your daughter. In reality she is losing her half sister. You cannot fix the problem, but you can help her grieve and you may be able to help the situation.

I suggest finding a DivorceCare for Kids (www.DC4K.org) group in your area. This is a wonderful program that helps children understand and process the losses experienced during divorce.

My next suggestion will require a loving and servant attitude that goes to a high level of sacrifice. You may need to work through these thoughts with a friend before implementing them, as it may take a little time to put aside any anger or frustration you may be experiencing. Keep as the main focus that you are doing this for your child. The very best thing for your daughter is for her to maintain a relationship with her sister.

I recommend calmly talking to your former spouse. It may be difficult, but refrain from becoming critical or aggressive. Instead, calmly share that your daughter is missing her sister. Inform him that you believe it is in the best interest of your daughter to have a relationship with her sibling.

The ideal situation is if the father is willing to have some of his visitation with both kids at the same time. However, if that isn't happening, then I would contact the mom and ask if she is open to the idea of the girls having a playdate together.

This could easily mean that you will be the one to do the babysitting and hard work. And I realize that doesn't sound reasonable or fair. However, the question isn't "What's fair?" but "What is best for my child?"

And in separation and divorce what's best for the kids is often extremely difficult for mom or dad and requires sacrifices.

Dear God,

I'm in a mess that's bigger than anything I could have imagined. I can't believe this is happening, but I find myself with the divorcee label—again! I thought another marriage would solve my problems, but I was wrong. I thought the first divorce was hard, but this is worse. I'm so embarrassed and ashamed that I don't know where to turn. I run to You, Lord.

I am broken in this world, but I desire to be whole before You. Lord, can You ever make me whole again? Help me to remember that another divorce does not change who I am. I am still Your beloved creation, the one that You love. I don't feel loved, but I stand on Your Word that I am loved. Jesus Christ paid the price for all of my sins, and I need forgiveness. I need You. My kids need You. My former spouse needs You. Heal us, Lord. Remove the shame.

Show me what to do next. I want to stop living life my way and do it only Your way. Light my path so that I do not stumble. And give me the courage, strength, and wisdom to keep walking even when I feel like giving up on life. Amen.

(Portions of this prayer are taken from John 3:16; 1 Thessalonians 1:4; 1 John 4:10; Psalms 119:105; and Isaiah 42:16.)

Chapter 12 Questions

1. Did you believe *The Brady Bunch* illusion before your second marriage? What about it seemed attractive? Did you assume you had learned from the mistakes in your first marriage?

2. What unresolved issues did you bring into the second marriage? What is the reason you did not take the time to heal those issues beforehand?

3. What were there warning signs that this marriage would be difficult? Did you ignore those signs?

4. What were the specific stress factors in your second marriage? How would your former spouse answer this question?

5. What are the similarities and differences between this marriage and divorce and the first one? What is surprising you about a second divorce?

6. How did your children feel about the remarriage? How do they feel about the divorce?

7. What are some specific steps you can take to recover from a second divorce?

8. Do you view another marriage as the answer to your pain? What can you do to help prevent another divorce?

To Do This Week …

- Offer to speak to the second marriage couples at the pre-marriage class at your church. Share with them the things you didn't realize would affect a second marriage.

13

I Can't Get No Satisfaction

SINGLE AND CONTENT

I don't like my voice. I don't like the way I look. I don't like the way I move. I don't like the way I act. I mean, period. So, you know, I don't like myself.

ELIZABETH TAYLOR

In 1971, rocker Mick Jagger bellowed the now-familiar phrase, "I can't get no satisfaction." You've got to give him credit; he was attempting every way possible to find what he was looking for. The song says he's riding around the world, yet the poor guy can't seem to find gratification anywhere.

In the Bible we read about King Solomon, who was on a similar quest for fulfillment. Using material possessions, information, creativity, money, food, drink, and sex, Mick and Solomon both strove to find satisfaction. Interestingly, both came up empty and frustrated!

In Ecclesiastes 1:2, Solomon roared, "Meaningless! Meaningless! … Utterly meaningless! Everything is meaningless!"

At first we might think, *this guy has got a bad attitude.* But does he? Could it be he's on to something profound? Could it be the human race experiences anxiety because we're searching for peace in

the wrong places? Where does a person find satisfaction in a world
that's so restless?

Psalm 63:5 (NLT) proclaims, "You [God] satisfy me more than the
richest feast. I will praise you with songs of joy." But is this realistic in
today's world? Can God really meet my needs as well as a piece of
Ghirardelli chocolate, a new boyfriend, or a red convertible?

People who find themselves single again aren't the only ones
searching for contentment. In each of the four seasons of my life—
single, married, divorced, and remarried—I've asked myself, *Why am
I discontent? What am I searching for?* Attempting to quench the rest-
lessness with shopping, eating, relationships, and accomplishments
proved futile. Finally, I investigated God's perspective on the subject.
Here is what I've found.

MY WORTH RESTS IN KNOWING AND BELIEVING I AM THE BELOVED

"You are precious and honored in my sight, and because I love
you" (Isa. 43:4).

Did you know God's love for you is so intense that He has your picture imprinted on His hands? Isaiah 49:16 (AB) says, "I have indelibly
imprinted (tattooed a picture of) you on the palm of each of My hands."
I spent the first ten years of my Christian life trying to earn God's love.
My pathetic and exhausting attempts were worthless. No matter how
many rungs on the ladder I climbed, I kept falling off. Each time I fell,
the enemy whispered, "You aren't very good at this Christian life, are you?
You are embarrassing yourself and God. It's too hard. You will always fail.
Why keep torturing yourself? Just give it all up." And I almost did.

Fortunately, I serve a God who relentlessly wooed me with His
zealous, unconditional love. My whole world changed, and I was sat-

urated with freedom and peace when I embraced the truth that I couldn't make Him love me any more or less. The tranquility I sought came in knowing not who I am, but *whose* I am. I'm the bride of Christ. This peace vanishes when I foolishly pursue other identities. It's in Him alone that I find my contentment and gratification. All satisfaction builds on this foundational fact: "In him we live and move and have our being" (Acts 17:28).

The Things That Matter to God Matter to Me

I grew up believing God was aloof, distant, and detached. I assumed He enjoyed being intimidating and was eager to zap me when I failed. Nothing could be further from the truth. God cares. The evidence of the Almighty's compassion is displayed in Psalm 56:8 (NLT): "You keep track of all my sorrows. You have collected all my tears in your bottle." God's love for His creation is so profound that He counts every tear.

In light of this I must ask, What about me? What stirs my compassion? Does God's lament bring sorrow to my own heart? Do I savor the things that delight Him? Do I care about others? If so, then my life has purpose. And when I have purpose, I have peace.

Several years ago, I visited the Wycliffe Bible Translators in England. While standing at a window at lunchtime, I saw children, age eight or nine, dash onto the playground. The variety of nationalities was fascinating. There were children from Asia, Africa, Europe, India, the United States, and the Middle East. Watching children of the world laugh, play, and hug each other brought me to tears. In that moment, God whispered, "I created each child, Laura. Their uniqueness and diversity is My design. I love each one—every single one." Immediately, my thoughts were transformed. I saw what He sees—His beloved. It took my breath away.

God has also used divorce-recovery ministry to teach me tenderness. Grieving with those who are suffering the trauma of divorce has given me sensitivity to their wounds. One of the seminar attendees will often comment, "I feel so much better just knowing that you recognize my pain. The hardest part is that no one seems to understand." Lifting their burden to God gives meaning to my own experience and brings fulfillment to my life.

God's goal is to make us like Christ. Jesus was deeply affected by and compassionate toward lost, wounded, broken, and abandoned people. Peace comes when my heart is undivided and I seek to live like Christ. My life has meaning and contentment when I'm doing the work of my Father. "I glorified You on the earth, having accomplished the work which You have given Me to do" (John 17:4 NASB).

I DESIRE A HUMBLE HEART

"O Lord, my heart is not conceited. My eyes do not look down on others. I am not involved in things too big or too difficult for me. Instead, I have kept my soul calm and quiet. My soul is content as a weaned child is content in its mother's arms" (Ps. 131:1–2 GW). Does this sound familiar? "Mirror, mirror on the wall, who's the fairest of them all?" It's a prevalent attitude found in America today, even in the church. Ironically, serenity usually arrives when I take my eyes off myself. My own reflection often fuels a hunger for adoration and recognition.

Would you like to test your sensitivity on this matter? Ask yourself a few questions: Am I obsessed with how and what everyone else is doing? Am I jealous when another person gets an impressive promotion, an attractive spouse (okay, any spouse), or stunning new clothes? Where does my mind automatically drift when I'm not thinking about something specific? Am I more concerned about my rights than my responsibilities?

A self-centered attitude defeats contentment and can keep us in the downward spiral of discouragement. Humility puts others first and halts the exhausting effort of focusing on ourselves.

In Scripture, we never see even a hint of Jesus being preoccupied with receiving glory or consumed about what others thought of Him. His focus was others rather than Himself. This rare attitude permeated the atmosphere around Him, and people were drawn to His ministry because of it. "Don't be selfish; don't try to impress others. Be humble, thinking of others as better than yourselves" (Phil. 2:3 NLT).

I Live More for Eternity Than for This World

Ecclesiastes states that we foolishly seek satisfaction "under the sun" (1:14), and herein lies the problem. We're looking in the wrong place. Satisfaction is found above the sun. The pleasure of heaven awaits us. Paradise is where we were created to live. It's home. So why do we act as though earth were our abode?

I believe the reason we keep such a firm grip on earth is that we have a misconception of heaven. For many people, the celestial wedding feast is envisioned in a dull, gray, church fellowship hall. The cuisine consists of a ham roll, a stalk of celery dipped in ranch dressing, and for Italians like me, a meatball—all served on a white paper plate. We shuffle around holding a white Styrofoam cup filled with lime-sherbet punch. A drab white cotton nightgown with huge white sleeves like a choir robe is our attractive attire. And if the person has been exceptionally holy, a gold sash may be added. (There's a lot of white in this picture, don't you think?)

We've got it all wrong. I believe heaven is going to be an enormous, lively reception. I'm talking bellyaching laughter, vibrant flowers, shimmering jewels, colors we have yet to imagine, singing and frolicking (remember David audaciously dancing before the ark of the covenant), and so much more.

Can you envision the worship team? Imagine Fanny Crosby, Rich Mullins, Charles Wesley, Point of Grace, Keith Green, and Beethoven all praising God at the same time! And guess who is sitting at the head table/throne? Jesus Himself. It's too much to fathom. I become giddy just thinking about it.

And don't forget the scrumptious non-caloric chocolate cake, topped with raspberry sauce and real whipped cream. Okay, I'm making that part up, but I'm dreaming big!

As if that weren't enough, now comes the superb part. Are you ready? Hold on. "And He will wipe away every tear from their eyes; and there shall no longer be any death; there shall no longer be any mourning, or crying, or pain; the first things have passed away" (Rev. 21:4 NASB). Did you catch that? No need for waterproof mascara—ever! No more cancer, guilt, gossip, bad breath, or dreary board meetings. I'm convinced that an accurate glimpse of heaven will make this life look pitiful.

This explains why it's so significant to spend our time here on earth preparing for eternity. "Teach us to live well! Teach us to live wisely and well!" (Ps. 90:12 MSG). A soothing peace floods our lives when we acquire a wise heart, and this gift assures us of the future. Wise hearts know the Redeemer lives, and He is waiting to caress us with heavenly pleasures. I don't know about you, but I can't wait!

I'm not certain what Mick Jagger is doing these days, but Ecclesiastes 12 explains Solomon's final evaluation. "The end of the matter is: Fear God [revere and worship Him, knowing that He is] and keep His commandments, for this is the whole of man [the full, original purpose of his creation, the object of God's providence, the root of character, the foundation of all happiness, the adjustment to all inharmonious circumstances and conditions under the sun] and the whole [duty] for every man" (v. 13 AB).

I know contentment can be found on earth, but I'm anticipating total joy in my celestial residence. I'm saturated with peace when I envision sitting on Christ's lap with my head nestled against His chest. I yearn for the moment when He tenderly lifts my chin and speaks deeply into my soul, "I love you, Laura. You are My cherished daughter and I delight in you. Your heart's desire is to be a good and faithful servant ... well done." Ah, now that, my friend, is true satisfaction.

"The master was full of praise. 'Well done, my good and faithful servant. You have been faithful in handling this small amount, so now I will give you many more responsibilities. Let's celebrate together!'" (Matt. 25:21 NLT).

Dear Lord,

I want my life to focus on You and what's really important. I want my heart to rejoice in the things that make You joyful, and I want to mourn over the things that make You sad. Society bombards me with its own standards, aspirations and cravings. I need You to replace those thoughts and desires with the truth that You alone can fulfill my deepest longings. Just give me Jesus. Let the rest fade away. Amen.

CHAPTER 13 QUESTIONS

1. Why do you think it's so hard to find satisfaction in our restless world?

2. Read Psalm 63:3–5. Can God really meet our deepest needs? Why, or why not? What things do people use to try to find contentment?

3. Where, according to the author, does life purpose come from?

4. If we really believe God cares about us, how will that influence how we live?

5. If God's goal is to make us like Christ, how might that truth influence how we respond to lost, wounded, broken, and/or abandoned people around us?

6. Do you seek to find your satisfaction in this world, or in the hope of eternity? Be honest! Why is it so easy to live as though earthly life is all there is?

7. What can we do to prepare for eternity? What light does Ecclesiastes 12:13 shed on this question?

8. Why do you think Isaiah 61:1–3 are some of the author's favorite verses? How might they relate to you?

To Do THIS WEEK ...

• Consider doing something you have never done before that will stir your creative juices, such as:

    ✓ Take an art or acting class.

    ✓ Learn a new sport or how to fly a kite.

    ✓ Join a writer's group.

    ✓ Create a model airplane.

    ✓ Build a house with Habitat for Humanity.

EPILOGUE

With This Ring, I Thee Wed

I will be with you always.

JESUS OF NAZARETH

"Your engagement ring is beautiful," the manicurist said.

"Thank you," I replied, attempting to still the butterflies that took flight every time I looked at it myself. "Today I add the wedding ring that matches it." In a few hours, my childhood dreams would be fulfilled and my hand would blissfully declare that I was a married woman.

My mind drifted to memories of when I was a teenager and another ring occupied the same finger—a lovely opal ring I received from my mother on my sixteenth birthday. "I also have an opal ring that I cherish," I explained, "but I lost it. I'd give anything to have it today as 'something old' for my wedding."

"Don't worry. These things have a way of turning up," she offered. "I bet you'll find it before the ceremony."

"I don't think so," I said, chuckling. Years of relentless searching for the ring had always yielded nothing.

Several years before, while traveling, I had wrapped the ring in a tissue and tucked it into my suede purse for protection. Upon arriving home, I rummaged through the purse for the ring, but it wasn't there.

After an hour of frantically searching every square inch of the purse—including ripping apart the lining—I had to accept the inevitable: The treasured ring was gone.

Over time, reminders of the ring would emerge, and I'd drag the purse out of the closet. I'd fervently search again while praying, "Dear God, I cherish this sweet-sixteen birthday present from my mom. As a single parent, this ring was a financial sacrifice for her. Please, I'm begging You—make it appear." But it never did.

Each hunt for the ring proved fruitless, so I would toss the old and worn purse into the trash, but within minutes I always retrieved it. My dream was that one day the ring would miraculously appear.

Examining my newly manicured nails, I turned my attention back to the present. "Soon I'll have a glittering wedding ring, and I'll never lose that one because it won't ever leave my finger." I smiled, content with the promise of what lay ahead rather than what was lost and behind me.

For a year and a half, married life was good. But the happiness was swiftly shattered when my husband announced that he wanted out of the marriage. Sorrow welled within me like a tidal wave, and the agony of removing my precious wedding ring was devastating. A barren hand was a constant reminder of my broken heart.

After weeping for months, I attempted to regain some normalcy by joining a friend on a shopping trip. That day, for some bizarre reason, I decided to use that old suede purse. I'm not certain why; perhaps it was a comforting reminder of sweeter times. I tossed my wallet, lipstick, and a few other items into the bag, and off we went.

While driving and chatting, I reached into the purse for a tissue. Feeling something strange inside the tattered tissue, imagine my shock when I saw my beloved opal ring! Bewildered and amazed, I laughed and cried at the same time. How did it get there? Why hadn't I found it before? I couldn't take my eyes off the ring. After years of hopeful searching, there it was. My friend watched in disbelief as she helped to keep the car on the road.

I slid the prized opal on my vacant, waiting finger. Like a mother tenderly drawing an injured child to her breast, the comfort of Jesus assured me, "I am betrothed to you forever. Others may desert you, but I'm your faithful Bridegroom. I will never abandon you. I have known since the beginning of time when your wounded heart would need this ring as a reassuring symbol of My love. I will never leave you, Laura, never."

During a time when I felt so worthless and unlovable, how fitting that God would choose a ring as the portrayal of His faithfulness and steadfast love.

When I get to heaven and Jesus bestows my crown on me, I wonder if it will be adorned with opals. Regardless, in humble gratitude I'll bow and lay those beautiful gems at His feet. "And when the Chief Shepherd appears, you will receive the unfading crown of glory" (1 Peter 5:4 NASB).

God isn't obligated to reveal Himself to us; He does it out of deep compassion. And His love is so intimate and personal that He may meet your need in a different way than He did mine. The point to remember is this: God is willing. Jesus Himself said, "I will not leave you as orphans; I will come to you" (John 14:18).

When I went through my divorce, the following Scripture passage furnished me with a desperately needed hope. "Keep your guard up. You're not the only ones plunged into these hard times. It's the same with Christians all over the world. So keep a firm grip on the faith. The suffering won't last forever. It won't be long before this generous God who has great plans for us in Christ—eternal and glorious plans they are!—will have you put together and on your feet for good" (1 Peter 5:9–10 MSG).

I would read it over and over for three reasons. First, it reminded me that I was not alone in my suffering. There was comfort in knowing others knew the same heartache. Second, it revealed God's promise of eventual relief from the sorrow. The words shed a desperately needed light at the end of my very dark tunnel. Third, it gave purpose to my pain and demonstrated that God had a plan for me.

It's my prayer that this book has provided you with that same type of reassurance and knowledge. You aren't alone. This season will pass. God will restore and strengthen your future.

When I embarked on divorce-recovery ministry, God provided a new Bible verse as a source of inspiration. These magnificent words serve me as a loyal companion. They prod me to persevere when I feel like giving up. If while reading this book you have received wisdom, conviction, or restoration; hope, consolation, or forgiveness, then Isaiah 61:1–3 has been fulfilled in my life. I'm forever grateful. I pray it will be a blessing to you as well:

> The Spirit of the Sovereign Lord is upon me, because the Lord has appointed me to bring good news to the poor. He has sent me to comfort the brokenhearted and to announce that captives will be released and prisoners will be freed. He has sent me to tell those who mourn that the time of the Lord's favor has come, and with it, the day of God's anger against their enemies. To all who mourn ... he will give beauty for ashes, joy instead of mourning, praise instead of despair. For the Lord has planted them like strong and graceful oaks for his own glory.

Someone I Love Is Divorcing

A GUIDE FOR FAMILY AND FRIENDS

A friend who can be silent with us in a moment of despair or confusion,
who can stay with us in an hour of grief and bereavement,
who can tolerate not knowing, not curing, not healing,
and face with us the reality of our powerlessness,
that is a friend who cares.

HENRI NOUWEN

If someone you love is divorcing, then you know all too well that the whole family is hit with a variety of emotions. The situation combines fear, shame, guilt, sorrow, and frustration into a fierce attack on those closest to the one divorcing. This unexpected inundation often causes friends and family members to withdraw into their own pain. Unfortunately, this response confirms in the mind of the one divorcing, "I'm an unlovable, disgraceful failure." Margaret Johnson shared some of the deepest emotions a mother feels in her book *Divorce Is a Family Affair.*[1] She wrote, "I knew that divorce across the nation was epidemic, and I was acutely aware of the tragic results of a broken home; but until now, until this very moment, I had thought of divorce as a misfortune that happened in other families, to other people. But now divorce was knocking on our door. This was our daughter, our grandchildren, our family."[1]

Not only did I experience a divorce, but my younger brother also divorced. Since I knew how it felt to have the world crumble at my feet, I was able to comfort him and reassure him that his emotions and fears were normal. But that didn't eliminate the profound grief in my own heart as I watched him suffer.

My brother, Mark, and I shared a tight bond while growing up. He was born very ill and almost died. Being the older sister, I developed a strong sense of protection toward him. As a child, I wouldn't let anyone hurt Mark, including the wicked doctor who attempted to give him his shots. I became so hysterical that my mother had to drag me from the examining room. And as we got older and he got into trouble, I couldn't endure him getting a spanking, so I'd confess to being the culprit and take the punishment he should have gotten. (Is it any wonder I became a rescuer?) As adults, the busyness of life caused us to drift apart, but during his divorce we talked almost every day.

Often we don't know what to do or say when someone close to us divorces. The following quotes are from family members as they share their perspective:

- "My older sister asked that I be there when her husband gathered his things to leave. She thought it best to have someone else present. Her concern was that he might take more than he should or have a serious reaction to the whole event. While I gladly agreed to help, it was quite an awkward situation."
- "When my brother divorced, I suffered a great sense of loss and sadness for him and myself. The loss of my sister-in-law caused me to feel a need to tuck away any affection for her

and try to remain neutral. I've stayed close to my nieces and nephew because their parents' divorce has had a devastating effect on them."

- "Supporting family members through divorce has been difficult because I watched them make unwise choices. So often I've wanted to say, 'Slow down! You have the next chapter of your life ahead of you. There's no rush.' But I knew they wouldn't listen."

- "It feels great to be needed during their difficult times, and it hurts when they move on."

- "We've struggled as parents with how to deal with the continued relationship we should or shouldn't have with our ex-daughter-in-law. It's difficult to deal with the anger we feel toward her and the pain we see our son and our grandchildren enduring."

- "It's killing us that we can't fix it. My child's pain is my pain, but I don't know what to do."

Friends and family often ask, "What can I do to help?" I've compiled a list of practical ways to help a loved one through separation or divorce. This list is broken into three categories: financial issues, children, and the emotional aspects of divorce. These bite-sized dos and don'ts come from many people who have been divorced.

FINANCIAL DOS AND DON'TS

Do

- Help your friend create an immediate crisis budget. If you aren't qualified to help, call your church and ask if an accountant, banker, or someone gifted with numbers would be willing to assist. If your church can't help, contact Crown Financial Ministries[2] to locate a local volunteer budget counselor.

- Assist your friend in finding affordable housing, or help her understand how to sell her house if she must vacate it.
- Be aware of immediate financial needs regarding attorney fees, childcare, and counseling.
- Buy a few bags of groceries or pay a utility bill.
- Help with car or house maintenance.
- Ask if she needs help paying for doctor/dental visits. Many people lose their health insurance during a divorce.
- Be aware of the children's enrollment in events that require a fee, such as karate or dance lessons. Then offer to pay for one or two sessions.
- Understand that the social life of your friend has drastically changed; therefore, treat him to dinner, a movie, or a football game.
- Fill the freezer with ready-made casseroles or easy-to-fix meals. Your loved one's concentration level is at an all-time low. One less thing to think about is an incredible blessing.
- Invite the family over for dinner.
- Help with the complicated research of finding a skilled lawyer.
- If employment is needed, check with friends, neighbors, and coworkers about potential job opportunities.
- Pay a portion of the fee for him or her to attend a divorce-recovery or single-parent seminar.
- Buy resource books that relate to your friend's situation. Many people would follow the counsel advised, but they can't afford to buy the books.

- These cheerful acts will communicate, "I'm thinking of you and I care."
- Surprise her with new bedroom linens, a comfortable pillow, and/or a nightgown. The greatest gift I got during my divorce was a pretty nightgown. It made me feel I was still a woman.
- Surprise him with small kitchen gadgets, appliances, dishes, lamps, and so forth.
- Offer a trip to a consignment shop. Some divorcing women must reenter the workforce after years of being at home. They may not have the wardrobe for a job interview.
- Delight him or her with morale boosters such as cards or small gifts.
- Give Christian worship music. This will help on those nights when your loved one is too weary to pray.

Don't

- Lend money unless you're okay with it never being paid back. Otherwise, it will put a strain on the relationship.
- Act offended if your friend doesn't seem grateful for your help. It may take time for him or her to recognize your sacrifice.
- Assume that because you're helping, you have the right to voice your opinion on their situation.

DOS AND DON'TS WITH CHILDREN

If I could reach the church with one message about children of divorce, it would be to tell them how desperate single parents are to have someone take an interest in their child's pain and suffering. It's the number one request I receive from single parents. Hear one mother as she shares her heartbreaking experience:

"My son was thirteen when my divorce was final. He really needed a Christian male influence in his life. A couple of men in our church would spend a lot of time talking to him at services. They'd promise to call him during the week, take him to events, and spend time with him. But they never followed through. This only added to his feeling that he couldn't trust Christian men. (His father headed a lay ministry.) After about two years of this, he refused to go to church and still is out of fellowship with God."

You don't need to travel to a distant land to minister to the poor and wounded. Lonely children are sitting right beside you in church. They need a man or woman to be a role model and comforter as their world spins out of control.

Here are some other suggestions:

Do

- Listen to them. Stop what you are doing and give them your full attention. A child or teen will share hidden fears or thoughts at unexpected times with a tender person who cares.
- Speak kindly and calmly to them. Their world is falling apart.
- Repeatedly assure them that the divorce isn't their fault.
- Offer to provide occasional childcare.
- Help the parent find a counselor who specializes in children's issues during divorce. Pay for a few visits if possible.
- Carpool or assist with transportation needs. With only one parent, who is probably working more than before the divorce, children often need a ride.
- Make homemade treats like cookies, casseroles, or fun food. Mom or Dad may be too busy or too broke for that now.

- Help children make Christmas or birthday gifts for both parents.
- Praise the strengths and gifts of both parents. "You're good at math, just like your dad."
- Provide a safe home where they can observe a healthy two-parent family. Include them in your family camping trips, outings, and so forth.
- Allow them to hold on to memories or items that have special meaning.
- Allow them to have responsibilities. This creates self-worth.
- Help them find an age-appropriate support group. DivorceCare for Kids is an excellent resource. See www.divorcecare.org/dc4k/

SPECIAL DOS AND DON'TS
FOR FAMILY MEMBERS

Do

- Provide children with pictures of when they were young. Help them recognize that they're treasured family members. Children need to hear stories about happier family times.
- Share old family photos and tell children funny stories about when you were young. Confirm that they're a part of a family heritage.
- Be a positive role model: Give of your time.

Don't

- Criticize either parent. If you already have, apologize.

- Lie. If they ask a question, give honest, age-appropriate answers. Always address the situation in question, don't attack the person.
- Forget that it takes two to five years for them to heal.
- Attempt to become the parent.
- Undermine the parents' authority.
- Be afraid to discipline within the parents' guidelines. Many single parents are too tired or afraid to discipline due to guilt. These kids are begging for boundaries that demonstrate love.
- Pump the children for information or ask them to spy on the other parent.
- Buy food, clothes, movies, or toys that intentionally anger either parent.
- Assume you know how the children are feeling.

EMOTIONAL DOS AND DON'TS

Do

- Be available. Make time for your friend or loved one.
- Find out the most difficult time of the week for her and keep her company. (Sundays are often the worst.)
- Stay conscious of her raw emotional state. Your friend will feel like a third wheel if she's the only single in a room full of couples.
- Recognize the stages of grief and understand they'll last for a while. Because divorce is so common, there's an incorrect assumption that people get over it quickly.
- LISTEN. Most people just want to know someone cares about their pain.

- Research names of excellent counselors who specialize in marital reconciliation, adultery, addictions, and/or codependency.

- Strongly encourage your loved one to attend a support group or offer to attend the first session with him, even if he doesn't want to go or doesn't think he needs it. The best healing takes place around others experiencing the same situation.

- Understand your loved one will be less likely to fall into the trap of a rebound relationship if she has a strong support system.

- Let your friend know he is loved unconditionally.

- Go to court or difficult events, such as weddings, funerals, or family gatherings with your loved one.

- Discern when you need to demonstrate "tough love." Get counsel from a divorce-recovery leader if you're uncertain.

- Listen for suicide threats.

- Pray night and day.

- Give your same-sex friend a hug. The bed is empty, the house cold. He or she needs human touch.

- Remember your friend with cards, letters, or flowers.

- Invite your loved one to church. Make sure to pick her up or meet in the parking lot and walk in together. Ask if she'd like a Bible.

- Invite your friend for the holidays. The first Christmas after a divorce is often the hardest.

- Help him put up decorations and take the children shopping for holidays.

- Remember your friend's birthday, and on her wedding anniversary help her to avoid depressing memories by spending the day together.

- Help church members understand your loved one's pain. Many churches will ostracize people when they divorce, even if it wasn't their choice.
- Reach out to the extended family of the one divorcing. They're hurting too.

DON'T

- Give advice unless he or she asks. (Exception: If there's child neglect or if the utilities are going to be turned off, you should share your concerns.)
- Drop out of sight because you don't know what to say or do.
- Share the details of your friend's situation with others.
- Assume you must pick sides. You can remain friends without turning against the other spouse.
- Judge. You have no way of knowing the pain this person might be experiencing.
- Criticize the spouse. Your friend may call him or her ugly names, but don't join in.
- Say, "Just get on with your life," or "There are other fish in the sea." These comments are well intentioned but bad advice.
- Take your loved one to movies that focus on the painful reality of divorce, children hurting, or romance. This creates more pain.
- Recite religious clichés such as, "God hates divorce and will make your spouse come back," or "God works all things for good." A better choice would be, "Laura, tell me what hurts the most and I'll pray for you. I know God loves you and longs to comfort you during this difficult time. I'm here for you."

- Fix them up with someone. Don't even think about it!
- Assume your friend still feels welcome at church. Subtle rejection can be more painful than the divorce itself. Many times those ostracized at church never recover and they leave for good.

APPENDIX B

Divorce Prevention

A GUIDE FOR PASTORS AND LEADERS

I believe that without realizing it, the church is contributing to the divorce rate in America. I know, I know—that's a radical statement. We typically view Christians as great promoters of marriage and family. The Bible holds marriage to be a sacred covenant, therefore we shudder at the thought that the church might actually exacerbate the problem of divorce. But what if it's true?

May I suggest an inventory of your own church? Using money, time, staff, resources, and volunteers as the measuring stick or litmus test, what is the value your church places on the following groups?

Singles—College and Career

Singles—Pre-Marriage

Single Parents

Single Again/Divorce Recovery

Stepfamilies

If yours is like most churches, it didn't score very high. When I lead workshops on this topic, attendees often drop their heads and slump into their seats. It's embarrassing to admit that the outreach to these groups is minimal if attempted at all. That's because the target audience for today's church is typically young married couples with children, which *can* help in divorce prevention. However, this attitude silently communicates that the ultimate goal for singles is to marry, and then they will "fit in" to the church. Until that time they are viewed as outsiders. The destructive aspect of this is that it can push singles into undesirable marriages too quickly. They may end up with mates who are emotionally unhealthy and spiritually immature at best, destructive and abusive at worst.

What is wrong with singleness? Why does the church unconsciously label singleness as synonymous with failure? Jesus, the one we call Savior and Lord, the one we worship, was—SINGLE!

This push to get everyone married has been around a long time. Can't you just see Jesus' friends Mary and Martha trying to fix Him up with the lady next door? "You don't know what You are missing, Jesus. Hannah is very pretty and her matzo ball soup is the best. Won't You at least *meet* her?" I can see Him chuckling and shaking His head thinking, *they just don't get it.* And unfortunately, neither do we.

Imagine if the church placed a high value on singleness and taught men and women to become content. What if a new pulpit perspective of singleness included: promoting it, celebrating it, treasuring it, and praising it? Would marriages last longer if we encouraged people to stay single until they were healed from past emotional wounds?

Based on my eighteen years in divorce-recovery ministry I believe the divorce rate would drop significantly if singles dealt with childhood pain and sinful choices before a relationship. However, I find very few churches that offer classes on these topics.

The remainder of this chapter is designed to help pastors and leaders reach out to these groups in an effort to prevent divorce. An entire chapter could be written on each topic. However, I have merely posed some aspects to consider.

SINGLES—COLLEGE AND CAREER

Of all the seasons in life, this one encompasses those who are making the most crucial decisions that affect adulthood. People at this stage complain, "I don't belong anywhere in the church. I'm too old for the teen group, and I don't fit in with the young couples. So, I stopped going to church." *USA Today* published an article on August 7, 2007, that stated, "Seven out of 10 Protestants ages 18-30, both evangelical and mainline, who went to church regularly in high school said they quit attending by age 23." A busy schedule of work, college, and dating is a significant reason they stop attending. However, I sense they are lonely and desire a place to belong that provides answers to some of life's perplexing questions.

This eighteen to thirty age range is frequently the time when people begin to search for a life partner. If a person isn't connected to a church that provides direction on how to identify emotional wounds, detect unsafe people, and recognize unhealthy relationships, it's easy to end up with a mate who isn't a wise choice. Who or what to worship is the most important decision in life, but who to marry is a close second.

Listed below are a few resources geared toward men and women in their twenties. These options and others in your local community may be helpful.

- Passion Conferences—Founded in 1997 under the direction of Louie Giglio, these conferences desire to bring a spiritual awakening to college campuses and are, "Committed to spreading the fame of Jesus Christ to the 16+ million college students of the nation and countless others around the globe." (www.268generation.com or e-mail info@268generation.com)

- Ivy Jungle College Network (www.IvyJungle.org)
- I Am Next—Campus Crusade (www.IAmNext.com)
- Relevant Magazine (www.RelevantMagazine.com)
- McLean Bible Church in Washington, DC—Frontline program (www.McLeanBible.org)

SINGLES—PRE-MARRIAGE

Pastor Scott Smith of Lakewood Baptist Church in Gainesville, Georgia, states, "Couples who ask me to marry them must commit to six weeks of intense pre-marital counseling. My goal over the course of our time together is to talk them out of marriage. I figure if I can do that, then most likely they shouldn't get married in the first place." He continues, "I attempt to uncover every possible landmine their relationship might encounter. It's my job to make it hard to get married, not easy. During these sessions I've had couples recognize major problems in their relationship and call off the wedding. I'd rather they separate 'this side of marriage' than on the other side. After 10 years of pre-marital counseling and having taken over 40 couples through this process, I've only had one couple divorce."

The couples fortunate enough to experience his pre-marriage counseling have a good chance for a thriving marriage. He requires each couple to read *Experiencing Christ Together* by Neil T. Anderson and Charles Mylander. In addition, they have to complete the "Prepare Inventory" at www.Prepare-Enrich.com.

If every pastor used this approach I believe we would have fewer divorces in the church. I once met an engaged woman who attended a large biblically based church. Curious to know what this church offered in the way of marriage preparation, I asked her. She replied, "Yes, we took that required class last week with a bunch of other couples. It was on a Saturday morning from 9 to noon." In this complex world, how can we convince ourselves that all the bride and groom need are a few "how to" tips?

My goal in this chapter is not to share pre-marriage resources, but to expose often overlooked issues that should be discussed before the ceremony. These are in addition to topics such as love, respect, communication skills, submission, common faith, intimacy, and "date nights," which are typically covered in pre-marriage sessions.

Many of the items on this list relate to past emotional wounds that often produce lingering shame. For example, my parents' divorce when I was eight years old produced long-term effects in me that went undiscovered for many years. When I became a Christian I assumed all the emotional consequences of that event were washed away with my sins. I was wrong. It wasn't until I was in my late thirties that I understood how my parents' breakup profoundly affected my life and my marriages. It's common for injured persons to convince themselves that issues have been dealt with, especially if they have forgiven past offenders. But if they haven't discovered how past pain influences their view of God, themselves, life and marriage it is a hidden and persistent ghost haunting the individual.

I am not recommending that intricate details be divulged during pre-marriage sessions. However, in certain circumstances professional counseling is needed.

Many divorces occur because the long-term consequences of past incidents were never addressed. Embarrassment may prevent couples from revealing the truth about sinful behaviors. It's critical that the counselor create an atmosphere of approachability and compassion, not condemnation. This is necessary if the couple is to grasp the pivotal point that both things done *to* us or *by* us accompany us into marriage. The pastor's job is to clearly communicate that the effects of past circumstances, if not addressed, can lurk in the shadows for many years, eating away at a marriage like cancer.

I am not implying that the pastor should do the counseling, but he or she must have a clear understanding of the topics noted in this chapter and how they can affect a marriage. Avoid the temptation of cliché answers such as "Just pray and forgive." Typically, these problems are deeply rooted and won't go away without professional help. If you as a pastor do not have a list of Christian counselors in your community, ask other pastors. They may know the names of those with the necessary training and skill to help people with difficult circumstances. Please research the names carefully. Bad counseling is worse than no counseling, and lay counselors often do not have the training to cope with the intensity of toxic issues.

In my speaking ministry I have a message entitled "The Quest For Happily Ever After—Revealing Truth About Relationships." Designed to help both singles and married couples, it explores many of the topics associated with divorce prevention. If you would like to know more about this workshop contact me at Laura@Laurapetherbridge.com.

This is a list of recommended topics to discuss during pre-marriage counseling. Please note if the couple is entering a remarriage, numerous additional issues should be included. The stepfamily section at the end of this book has resources listed.

You may need training to detect if someone has experienced one of these issues but is in denial about the problem. A local counselor can advise you on how to obtain that instruction.

- Sexual Abuse—Did the person receive professional help? Are issues still remaining?
- Abuse or Emotional Wounds During Childhood—This topic includes violence, neglect, abandonment, alcoholism, or substance abuse by anyone in the home, intense criticism, being forced into an adult role, parents either emotionally or legally divorced, and mentally ill or physically disabled parents.
- Pre-Marital Sex—Have the consequences been discussed?
- Sexually Transmitted Diseases—Does either party have one? Has it been discussed? Has a previous disease caused infertility?
- Abortion—Was proper counseling obtained? (Both men and women need to grieve an abortion.) Does guilt or shame remain? Is the effect it could have on raising children understood?
- Homosexuality—Have all tendencies been discussed?
- Pornography—Is there presently or has there been activity in this area? Is its destructive effect clearly understood? (Many couples incorrectly assume pornography usage will disappear once they marry; the opposite is often the case.)
- Past and Present Drug or Alcohol Usage—Do you know how to detect overindulgence or addiction?
- Anger or Violence—Has the couple learned to fight fair? Has there been ANY incidence of physical violence including physical restraint, shoving or slapping?

- Parents—What dysfunctions were present in each home growing up? How involved will the parents be in the marriage? (Counselees may need prompting to understand underlying problems because the patterns feel normal.)
- Selfishness—Was either party indulged or sheltered a great deal? Do they possess an "I deserve to be happy" mentality?
- Finances—Is either party in significant debt? What are the spending habits? Does either person feel financially responsible for extended family members?
- Children—Do both parties desire to have children? (Give permission to tell the truth, particularly to the male.) What is their view of proper discipline?
- Pets—What will happen to pets once the couple marry? What about when children come along?

SINGLE PARENTS

Does the Bible have instruction to the church about parents without a spouse? When you hear the word *widow* what comes to mind? Typically, we think of a woman who has lost a husband to death. However, the term is more all-encompassing. Larry Burkett's *Single Parent Manual,* coauthored by Brenda Armstrong, states, "Webster's definition of the phrase includes, 'Grass Widow,' which includes a woman that has never been married, divorced or separated. The Bible uses a similar definition in James 1:27. The word, 'Chera' (Khay-rah), means 'grass widow' which is interpreted as the idea of deficiency; a widow (as lacking a husband), literal or figurative."[1] This means that God has compassion for all single parents, not only those who have experienced the death of a spouse. For years the church has been unaware or unwilling to reach out to this group. Fortunately, some churches are recognizing the need for help.

Single parents have a wide range of fundamental needs, including childcare, safe and affordable housing, food, clothing, and transportation. In addition, they may require medical and dental care, baby supplies, counseling, and a job or more education. They must attend to all the tasks and responsibilities typically covered by two people. When you factor in the loneliness and the stress of disciplining children, you have a prime breeding ground for landing in a bad relationship. Women more often seek out a mate for financial relief and help with unruly children. Men seek companionship and a way back to the "normal family."

Predators or unstable people can spot a vulnerable person quickly. They often target defenseless single mothers with the sole intention of victimizing the children. Therefore, it's crucial for the church to reach out and protect this vulnerable group.

God acknowledges that single parents can easily be exposed to danger. James 1:27 informs the church, "Religion that God our Father accepts as pure and faultless is this: to look after orphans and widows in their distress and to keep oneself from being polluted by the world." God knows that if single parents find community, assistance and support from the local church they are less likely to end up the target of domestic violence or in circumstances that may place their kids at risk.

There are excellent Christian resources available to assist the church in ministering to single parents. Here are a few of my favorites:

- *New Start for Single Moms* by Diane Strack
- *Successful Single Parenting* by Gary Richmond
- *The Single Dad's Survival Guide* by Michael Klumpp

- *Financial Relief for Single Parents* by Brenda Armstrong
- *A Single Mom's Guide to Finding Joy in the Chaos* by Elsa Kok Colopy (Geared for women with young children.)

SINGLE AGAIN—DIVORCE RECOVERY

A familiar misconception about divorce-recovery ministry is that it will encourage people to get divorced. Some church leaders feel that creating a support system for those experiencing divorce subtly communicates that it's a good thing to walk out on your spouse. Nothing could be further from the truth.

For those who have this false impression I say attend one session of a group and see for yourself. If facilitated properly, the experience will immediately eradicate fears and misconceptions. This is a group of weeping, grieving, devastated people. It's not a party. It's a funeral. Typically, the spouse who didn't want the marriage to end is the one who attends a divorce-recovery support group. It's a safe place to unload anger, fear, and loneliness that accompany the death of a marriage.

Divorce-recovery ministry is a hidden mission field. Many people who had no desire to attend church before a divorce are willing to participate in a support group afterward. In the pit of despair many encounter God for the first time. Finding in Him the love they searched for in a spouse, they learn from God the meaning of forgiveness and begin to trust the only one who is eternally faithful.

One of the surprising things that can occur when a church offers a divorce support group is the attendees become more emotionally and spiritually mature than they were prior to the divorce. They learn parenting skills and find their identity in Christ rather than in a spouse. This is why divorce-recovery ministry increases the survival rate of second marriages.

A common phrase I hear from those who attend a divorce-recovery group or seminar is, "I was in total despair and didn't want to go on. This saved my life. Thank you for being there for me. I'll never forget it." If that isn't Jesus with skin on I don't know what is.

STEPFAMILIES

The TV show *The Brady Bunch* was a lie. It led us to believe that blending two families is an easy, fun, and smooth process. It isn't. I've had two stepmothers and now I am a stepmother, and I can assuredly say the transition is neither easy nor smooth.

Often churches assume that stepfamilies are dealing with the same issues as biological families, and they are. But stepfamilies have additional stressors that make life much, much more complicated.

Typically, there is at least one former mate to contend with, plus previous in-laws, visitation schedules, child-support payments, kids screaming, "You aren't my father, you can't tell me what to do," and—well, you get the picture.

Why don't we see more workshops in churches geared to the multi-faceted issues associated with stepfamilies? A big reason is that stepfamilies pretend they are biological families. They work very hard not to stand out, to convince themselves and others they aren't different. This is a huge mistake. Ignoring the complex dynamics of a stepfamily sets a marriage up for failure.

Therefore, if the church desires to decrease the divorce rate in second marriages it must communicate that stepfamilies have unique needs. Conducting pre-marriage classes and ongoing workshops on topics associated with stepfamilies works well. The leadership should be educated on the complex issues they face.

Here are a few excellent resources:

- *The Smart Stepfamily* by Ron L. Deal (books, tapes, and seminars)
- *Tying the Family Knot* by Terri Clark
- *Raising Children in Blended Families* by Maxine Marsolini
- *Saving Your Second Marriage Before It Starts* by Les and Leslie Parrott

I pray these suggestions help you understand how the church can decrease the divorce rate by recognizing and ministering to groups of people in the church who are often overlooked.

APPENDIX C

Divorce-Recovery Ministry

A GUIDE FOR PASTORS AND LEADERS

The U.S. Census Bureau reported in 2006 that almost 20 million Americans—about 9.9 percent of the U.S. population—are currently divorced. As the church, we cannot afford to "close our eyes and hope it goes away." We need to open our doors and our arms to those who are hurting from the pain of divorce, and welcome them with God's love and grace.

In the previous appendix on divorce prevention I explained how divorce-recovery ministry can be the entry point into the church for a hurting individual. If our sincere heart's desire is to be the hands and feet of Jesus Christ, and if we believe He is the answer to every need, then we need to create a safe place for emotionally wounded men and women who are experiencing separation or divorce. They seek a way to find hope, healing, and restoration. The question is, will the church be the place they find solace or must they turn to the local bar to ease the pain? Will the church continue to communicate that the blood of Christ is not powerful enough to cover divorce, or will we proclaim that Jesus, the true Lover of our souls, has the ability to heal any wound, sin, or sorrow?

If you desire to reach out to others through a divorce-recovery ministry, here are a few suggestions on how to begin. This book can be used in a support-group setting by using the questions available at the end of each chapter to facilitate. There are other products listed in the resource section of this book, including DivorceCare (www.DivorceCare.org).

You will need to provide childcare; single parents often have no financial resources or family to watch the children while they attend. An even better idea would be to include a program for children such as DivorceCare for Kids (www.DC4K.org).

There are a handful of general guidelines that may help you to detect who would be the best person to implement and facilitate a divorce-recovery program in your church. The following are the leadership qualities that I recommend:

- *Compassionate.* The person must possess a genuine heart for those who are struggling and/or grieving. A hurting person can detect a "just get over it" or "stop whining" careless attitude. This callous demeanor destroys the trust factor (John 13:35).
- *Concerned about people, not a program.* Although the ability to stay on task is vitally important when leading a group, it should never become more valuable than allowing people to grieve and share their situation (Isa. 57:18).
- *Restored.* A facilitator who displays bitterness, revenge, or an obsession about his or her own issues clearly is not ready to lead others (1 Peter 4:14).

- *Spiritually stable.* This person must possess sensitivity toward God, the ability to share his or her own salvation experience, and a general knowledge of Biblical accuracy (Job 12:13).

- *Recognizes the difference between mercy and rescuing.* A healthy leader has dealt with his or her own co-dependency issues and realizes it is not the job of the facilitator to "fix" the other person's problems. The role is to listen, encourage, and say no without guilt when necessary (Prov. 28:5; Matt. 18:15-18).

- *Teachable.* Benjamin Franklin was right: "A man who will not follow should not lead." If the person feels he or she already knows all the answers it's doomed (John 16:13).

- *Servant.* A controlling leader can destroy a group. Jesus is our role model, and He never led by manipulating others. "I am gentle and humble" (Matt. 11:29).

- *Available.* It is not wise if a facilitator is overly committed to several other ministries or activities. This should be the primary ministry (Col. 3:23, 4).

- *Good Listener.* If the facilitator dominates the conversation or takes the group down "rabbit trails," he or she isn't ready to lead (James 1:26).

- *Confidential.* Delicate things are often disclosed in this group. If a facilitator repeats outside the group what was shared inside, it will have a disastrous affect (Ps. 141:3).

- *Willing to Receive Constructive Criticism.* A mature person realizes this is necessary for growth (Prov. 27:17).

- *A Team Player.* A "Lone Ranger" or this is "my" ministry mentality will be damaging for the group (John 17:21).

- *Pure.* If a person struggles with immorality or pornography
  he or she will need to conquer that battle before becoming
  a facilitator (Prov. 28:13).

Once you have obtained facilitators it's important for them to observe or participate in a divorce-recovery support group before leading one. Ask local counselors, pastors, or nearby churches for information, or check the DivorceCare Web site. A support group is only as safe, healthy, and stable as the facilitator.

When your facilitators are ready to begin and childcare is in place, advertise in the church bulletin. Because you don't want to overload the first group, I don't recommend opening it up to the community unless your church is small. As the facilitators become more knowledgeable, advertising in strategic places such as with lawyers and doctors, newspapers, and other churches will help the ministry to grow. To reach those in the community I suggest hanging a banner in front of the church.

A consistent attendance of ten to twelve people signifies that it's time to launch a second group. Those who graduated from the group, and took the time and made the commitment to fully recover, often make the best leaders.

Even though many participants desire to date immediately, I encourage them to wait at least two years after a divorce to begin a new relationship. Therefore, I recommend offering a small group or Bible study as a follow up to the support group. This should be equipped with resources and topics that focus on helping them to become emotionally stable. I strongly advise against sending the participants into singles ministry where the focus is often on finding "Mr. or Mrs. Right."

In this short appendix it is impossible to cover all of the significant issues associated with divorce-recovery ministry. I conduct a one-day facilitator training where I share the wise and foolish things that I have learned in my eighteen years of divorce-recovery ministry. If you would like details please contact me via www.LauraPetherbridge.com.

It is my prayer that this information and book have inspired you to reach out to those who are brokenhearted due to separation or divorce.

Resources

Each of these resources, listed by category, can provide helpful information. However, this doesn't mean I endorse or agree with everything written in them.

CHILDREN/ADULT CHILDREN OF DIVORCE

Jen Abbas, *Generation Ex: Adult Children of Divorce and the Healing of Our Pain* (Little Rock, AR: Family Life, 2007). Go to www.JenAbbas.com for excellent articles and information on adult children of divorce.

Archibald D. Hart, *Children and Divorce* (Dallas: Word, 1985).

Archibald D. Hart, *Growing Up Divorced* (Ann Arbor, MI: Servant, 1994).

Kids Hope, Gary Sprague president and founder, PO Box 6020, Woodland Park, CO 80866, 1-888-kids-hope (1-888-543-74670 www.KidsHope.org

Elizabeth Marquardt, *Between Two Worlds* (New York: Crown, 2005).

Tom and Beverly Rodgers, *Adult Children of Divorced Parents: Making Your Marriage Work* (San Jose, CA: Resource Publications, 2002). (This book is self-published. To obtain copies visit www.acodp.com.

Judith Wallerstein, Julia Lewis, and Sandra Blakeslee, *The Unexpected Legacy of Divorce* (New York: Hyperion, 2001).

Thomas A. Whiteman, *Your Kids and Divorce* (Grand Rapids, MI: Revell, 2001).

CODEPENDENCY

Dan B. Allender, *Bold Love* (Colorado Springs: NavPress, 1992).

Melody Beattie, *Codependent No More* (New York: HarperCollins, 1992).

Celebrate Recovery: Christian recovery program on how to become free from addictive, compulsive, and dysfunctional behaviors. www.CelebrateRecovery.com

Henry Cloud and John Townsend, *Boundaries in Marriage* (Grand Rapids, MI: Zondervan, 1999).

James Dobson, *Love Must Be Tough* (Wheaton, IL: Tyndale, 1994).

DEVOTIONALS

Bonnie Bruno, *When God Steps In* (Cincinnati, OH: Standard, 2007).

Steve Grissom and Kathy Leonard, *Divorce Care* (Nashville: Nelson, 2006).

Linda W. Rooks, *Broken Heart on Hold* (Colorado Springs: David C. Cook, 2006).

Rose Sweet, *Healing the Divorced Heart* (Chattanooga, TN: AMG International, 2003).

Kari West, *Dare to Trust, Dare to Hope Again* (Colorado Springs: David C. Cook, 2001).

RECOVERY

Alcoholics Anonymous, PO Box 459, New York, NY 10163, 212-870-3400, www.alcoholics-anonymous.org

Cocaine Anonymous, 3740 Overland Ave., Suite C, Los Angeles, CA 90034, 1-800-347-8998, www.ca.org

DivorceCare, PO Box 1739, Wake Forest, NC 27588, 1-800-489-7788, www.DivorceCare.org

Domestic Violence Hotline 1-800-799-SAFE (7233).

Grace Fox, *Moving From Fear to Freedom* (Eugene, OR: Harvest House, 2007).

Gamblers Anonymous, PO Box 17173, Los Angeles, CA 90017, 213-386-8789, www.gamblersanonymous.org

Jim Smoke, *Growing Through Divorce* (Eugene, OR: Harvest House, 1995).

Rose Sweet, *A Woman's Guide to Healing the Heartbreak of Divorce* (Peabody, MA: Hendrickson, 2001).

Bob Burns and Tom Whiteman, *The Fresh Start Divorce Recovery Workbook* (Nashville: Nelson, 1992, 1998). www.FreshStartSeminars.org 1-888-373-7478.

FINANCIAL/LEGAL

Crown Financial Ministries, 601 Broad Street SE, Gainesville, GA 30501, 1-800-722-1976. www.Crown.org

Joseph Warren Kniskern, *When the Vow Breaks* (Nashville: Broadman and Holman, 2008).

GRIEF ISSUES

Mark Atteberry, *Walking with God on the Road You Never Wanted to Travel* (Nashville: Nelson, 2005).

M. Craig Barnes, *When God Interrupts* (Downers Grove, IL: InterVarsity, 1996).

Archibald Hart and Catherine Hart Weber, *Unveiling Depression in Women* (Grand Rapids, MI: Baker, 2001).

Les Carter, *The Anger Workbook* (Nashville: Nelson, 1992).

Tim Hansel, *Dancin' Toward the Dawn* (Colorado Springs: David C. Cook, 2000).

David Hazard, *When You Can't Say "I Forgive You"* (Colorado Springs: NavPress, 2000).

Lauren Littauer Briggs, *The Art of Helping* (Colorado Springs: David C. Cook, 2003).

Ben Patterson, *Waiting—Finding Hope When God Seems Silent* (Downers Grove, IL: InterVarsity, 1991).

Lewis Smedes, *Forgive and Forget: Healing the Hurts We Don't Deserve* (New York: HarperOne, 2007)

Charles Swindoll, *Encourage Me* (Grand Rapids, MI: Zondervan, 1993).

H. Norman Wright, *Recovering from Losses in Life* (Grand Rapids, MI: Revell, 2006).

Leslie Vernick, *Getting Over the Blues* (Eugene, OR: Harvest House, 2005).

RECONCILIATION/BIBLICAL INSIGHTS ON DIVORCE

Gary Chapman, *Hope for the Separated* (Chicago: Moody Press, 2005).

Tim Clinton, *Before a Bad Goodbye* (Nashville: Nelson, 1999).

Myles Munroe, *Single, Married, Separated, and Life After Divorce*
(Shippensburg, PA: Destiny Image, 1993).

Sexual Abuse

Dan B. Allender, *The Wounded Heart* (Colorado Springs: NavPress,
1995).

Jan Coates, *Set Free* (Enumclaw, WA: WinePress Publishing, 2007).

Jan Frank, *Door of Hope* (Nashville: Nelson, 1995).

Hart Institure, Catherine Hart Weber and Archibald Hart,
www.HartInstitute.com.

Diane Mandt Langberg, *On the Threshold of Hope: Opening the Door
to Healing for Survivors of Sexual Abuse* (Carol Stream, IL:
Tyndale House, 1999).

Leslie Vernick, *The Emotionally Destructive Relationship: Seeing It,
Stopping It, Surviving It* (Eugene, OR: Harvest House, 2007).
www.LeslieVernick.com

Sexual Addiction/Homosexuality

Exodus International. Help for those with unwanted same-sex attrac-
tions. PO Box 540119, Orlando, FL 32854, 1-888-264-0877,
www.Exodus-International.org.

Kathy Gallagher, *When His Secret Sin Breaks Your Heart* (Dry Ridge,
KY: Pure Life Ministries, 2003).

Mike Haley, *101 Frequently Asked Questions About Homosexuality*,
(Eugene, OR: Harvest House, 2004).

Laurie Hall, *An Affair of the Mind* (Wheaton, IL: Tyndale, 1998).

Love in Action, PO Box 280386, Memphis, TN 38168, 1-800-201-
4129, www.LoveInAction.org

Marsha Means, *Living with Your Husband's Secret Wars* (Grand
     Rapids, MI: Revell, 1999).
New Life Partners, PO Box 970638, Boca Raton, FL 33497,
     www.NewLifePartners.org.
Harry Schaumburg, *False Intimacy* (Colorado Springs: NavPress,
     1992), www.SexualWholeness.com
Doug Weiss, Heart to Heart Conseling Center, confidential tele-
     phone counseling, 1-719-278-3708, www.SexAddict.com.
Anita Worthen and Bob Davies, *Someone I Love Is Gay* (Downers
     Grove, IL: InterVarsity, 1996).

SINGLE LIFE/DATING/SEXUALITY

Stephen Arterburn and Meg J. Rinck, *Avoiding Mr. Wrong* (Nashville:
     Nelson, 2001).
Lisa Bevere, *Kissed the Girls and Made Them Cry* (Nashville: Nelson,
     2002).
Henry Cloud and John Townsend, *Safe People* (Grand Rapids, MI:
     Zondervan, 1995).
Rob Eagar, *Dating with Pure Passion* (Eugene, OR: Harvest House,
     2005).
Patti Gordon, *Press Play* (Sisters, OR: Multnomah, 2006).
Thomas Jones, *The Single-Again Handbook* (Nashville: Nelson,
     1993). www.FreshStartSeminars.org
Dick Purnell, *Finding a Lasting Love* (Eugene, OR: Harvest House,
     2003).
Mary Whelchel, *Common Mistakes Singles Make and How to Avoid
     Them* (Grand Rapids, MI: Revell, 2008).

SINGLE PARENTING

Brenda Armstrong, *Financial Relief for Single Parents* (Chicago: Moody Publishers, 2007).

Brenda Armstrong, *The Single Mom's Workplace Survival Guide* (Ann Arbor, MI: Servant, 2002).

Robert G. Barnes Jr., *Single Parenting* (Wheaton, IL: Living Books, 1992).

Elsa Kok Colopy, *The Single Mom's Guide to Finding Joy in the Chaos* (Grand Rapids, MI: Revell, 2006).

Gary Richmond, *Successful Single Parenting* (Eugene, OR: Harvest House, 1998).

Diane Strack, *New Start for Single Moms* (Nashville: Nelson, 2007).

SPIRITUAL GROWTH

There are so many incredible books to choose from. Here are a few of my favorites.

Fil Anderson, *Running on Empty* (Colorado Springs: WaterBrook, 2005).

John Eldredge, *The Journey of Desire* (Nashville: Nelson, 2001).

John Eldredge, *Waking the Dead* (Nashville: Nelson, 2006).

Elizabeth George, *Loving God with All Your Mind* (Eugene, OR: Harvest House, 2005).

Beth Moore, *Breaking Free* (Nashville: Broadman and Holman, 2000).

Henri J. M. Nouwen, *The Return of the Prodigal Son* (New York: Doubleday, 1994).

John Ortberg, *The Life You've Always Wanted* (Grand Rapids, MI: Zondervan, 2002).

Rick Warren, *The Purpose Driven Life* (Grand Rapids, MI: Zondervan, 2007).

Philip Yancey, *What's So Amazing About Grace?* (Grand Rapids, MI: Zondervan, 2002).

STEPFAMILY

Terri Clark, *Tying the Family Knot* (Nashville: Broadman and Holman, 2004).

Ron L. Deal, *The Smart Stepfamily* (Bloomington, MN: Bethany House, 2002). http://www.successfulstepfamilies.com/

Maxine Marsolini, *Raising Children in Blended Families* (Grand Rapids, MI: Kregel, 2006).

Notes

Chapter 2

1. Beth Moore, *Praying God's Word* (Nashville: Broadman and Holman, 2000).

Chapter 3

1. *Atlanta Journal Constitution*, Feb. 14, 2003, "Living Section."

2. Judith Wallerstein, Julia M. Lewis, and Sandra Blakeslee, *The Unexpected Legacy of Divorce* (New York: Hyperion, 2001), 33–34.

3. Gary Sprague, "Five Foundational Principles for Single Adults," single parent family Web site, www.spfm.org.

4. Gary Richmond, *Successful Single Parenting* (Eugene, OR: Harvest House, 1998).

5. James Dobson, *Preparing for Adolescence* (Ventura, CA: Gospel Light, 2005).

6. Robert G. Barnes Jr., *Single Parenting* (Wheaton, IL: Living Books, 1992), 210–211.

Chapter 5

1. Philip Yancey, *What's So Amazing About Grace?* (Grand Rapids, Mich.: Zondervan, 1997), 85.

2. Ibid, 115.

3. Judi Reid, advocate against pornography and sexual addiction, PO Box 29721, Richmond, VA 23242, 1-804-740-2403, JudiGReid@aol.com.

4. T. W. Hunt, *The Mind of Christ* (Nashville: Broadman and Holman, 1997).

5. Henry Cloud and John Townsend, *Boundaries* (Grand Rapids, MI: Zondervan, 2002).

Chapter 6

1. Bob Burns and Tom Whiteman, *The Fresh Start Divorce Recovery Workbook* (Nashville: Nelson, 1998), 140.

2. Joseph Warren Kniskern, *When the Vow Breaks* (Nashville: Broadman and Holman 2008), chapters 12, 13, and 14.

3. Crown Financial Ministries, PO Box 100, Gainesville, GA 30503, 1-800-722-1976, www.Crown.org.

4. Ibid.

5. Mike Haley, *101 Frequently Asked Questions About Homosexuality* (Eugene, OR: Harvest House, 2004).

Chapter 7

1. Pat Springle, *Rapha's Twelve-Step Program for Overcoming Codependency* (Houston and Dallas: Rapha, 1990), 13.

2. John P. Splinter, *The Complete Divorce Recovery Handbook* (Grand Rapids, MI: Zondervan, 1992), 83.

3. Henry Cloud and John Townsend, *Boundaries in Marriage* (Grand Rapids, MI: Zondervan, 1999), 227.

Chapter 8

1. Gary Richmond, *Successful Single Parenting* (Eugene, OR: Harvest House, 1998).

Chapter 12

1. E. Mavis Hetherington is professor emeritus, Department of Psychology, University of Virginia. *For Better or For Worse: Divorce Reconsidered,* Dr. Hetherington specifies the divorce rate for stepcouples to be "50 percent higher in remarriages with stepchildren" (New York: Norton, 2003; p. 178). The Virginia Longitudinal study does not consist of a nationally representative sample but is a broader representation of step-families in America than other previous research. J. Larson (1992), "Understanding Stepfamilies," *American Demographics,* 14, 360.

2. F. F. Furstenburg, (1987), *The New Extended Family.* In K. Pasley and M. Ihinger-Tallman (eds.), *Remarriage and Stepparenting: Current Research and Theory* (p. 42-64), New York: Guilford). Reported in Susan Stewart, *Brave New Stepfamilies,* 2007.

3. James Dobson, *Bringing Up Boys* (Carol Stream, IL: Tyndale, 2005), 136.

4. Lawerence H. Ganong and Marilyn Coleman, *Stepfamily Relationships,* (New York: Springer, 2003).

Appendix A

1. Margaret Johnson, *Divorce Is a Family Affair* (Grand Rapids, MI: Zondervan, 1983), 11.

2. Crown Financial Ministries, PO Box 100, Gainesville, GA 30503, 1-800-722-1976, www.Crown.org.

Appendix B

1. Crown Financial Ministries, *Single Parent Ministry Training Manual*, 13.